# CITYSPOTS
# GENE

## WHAT'S IN YOUR GUIDEBOOK?

**Independent authors** Impartial up-to-date information from our travel experts who meticulously source local knowledge.

**Experience** Thomas Cook's 165 years in the travel industry and guidebook publishing enriches every word with expertise you can trust.

**Travel know-how** Thomas Cook has thousands of staff working around the globe, all living and breathing travel.

**Editors** Travel-publishing professionals, pulling everything together to craft a perfect blend of words, pictures, maps and design.

**You, the traveller** We deliver a practical, no-nonsense approach to information, geared to how you really use it.

# CITYSPOTS
# GENEVA

**Written by Kerry Walker**
**Updated by Anna Ridley**

**Published by Thomas Cook Publishing**
A division of Thomas Cook Tour Operations Limited
Company registration No: 3772199 England
The Thomas Cook Business Park, 9 Coningsby Road
Peterborough PE3 8SB, United Kingdom
Email: books@thomascook.com, Tel: +44 (0)1733 416477
www.thomascookpublishing.com

**Produced by The Content Works Ltd**
Aston Court, Kingsmead Business Park, Frederick Place
High Wycombe, Bucks HP11 1LA
www.thecontentworks.com

Series design based on an original concept by Studio 183 Limited

ISBN: 978-1-84848-135-0

First edition © 2007 Thomas Cook Publishing
This second edition © 2009 Thomas Cook Publishing
Text © Thomas Cook Publishing
Maps © Thomas Cook Publishing/PCGraphics (UK) Limited
Transport map © Communicarta Limited

Series Editor: Lucy Armstrong
Production/DTP: Steven Collins

Printed and bound in Spain by GraphyCems

Cover photography (The *Broken Chair* sculpture in the gardens of the
Palais des Nations) © imagebroker/Alamy

All rights reserved. No part of this publication may be reproduced, stored in a retrieval
system or transmitted, in any form or any means, electronic, mechanical, recording
or otherwise, in any part of the world, without prior permission of the publisher.
Requests for permission should be made to the publisher at the above address.

Although every care has been taken in compiling this publication, and the contents
are believed to be correct at the time of printing, Thomas Cook Tour Operations
Limited cannot accept any responsibility for errors or omission, however caused,
or for changes in details given in the guidebook, or for the consequences of any
reliance on the information provided. Descriptions and assessments are based on
the author's views and experiences when writing and do not necessarily represent
those of Thomas Cook Tour Operations Limited.

# CONTENTS

## SYMBOLS KEY

The following symbols are used throughout this book:

ⓐ address   ☎ telephone   ⓦ website address   ⓔ email
🕒 opening times   Ⓝ public transport connections   ❶ important

The following symbols are used on the maps:

| | | | |
|---|---|---|---|
| 𝒊 | information office | ▪ | points of interest |
| ✈ | airport | ◯ | city |
| ✚ | hospital | ◯ | large town |
| 🛡 | police station | ◦ | small town |
| 🚌 | bus station | = | motorway |
| 🚆 | railway station | — | main road |
| Ⓜ | metro | — | minor road |
| ✝ | cathedral | — | railway |
| ❶ | numbers denote featured cafés & restaurants | | |

Hotels and restaurants are graded by approximate price as follows:
£ budget price   ££ mid-range price   £££ expensive

◗ *Geneva's giant Floral Clock*

# Introduction

Geneva is like a huge Swiss chocolate box, where each experience should be savoured: from the hum of life in the medieval Old Town to the pin-drop peace of the lakefront, where the early morning mist peels back to reveal Mont Blanc. On the surface this city is silky smooth, with its 5-star hotels, plush boutiques and gourmet haunts – but appearances can be deceptive. Bite beneath the surface and you'll get an explosion of different experiences.

Most surprising, perhaps, is the proximity of nature to the city, and the variation of its forms. Within spitting distance of the mighty UN headquarters, you can take a ride across Europe's largest alpine lake, its contours carved out by glaciers, sip home-grown Pinot Noirs in vine-clad Satigny, spot pink flamingoes in the Jardin Botanique and whoosh down the French Alps on a pair of skis. And with promenades hugging the water's edge, this is one place you won't want to be without your walking boots.

This city of 186,000 inhabitants may be small, but it thinks big. The Cathédrale St Pierre towers above the cobbled Old Town, the 140 m (460 ft) Jet d'Eau fountain creates a rainbow with its spray and the enormous Horloge Fleurie (Floral Clock) raises eyebrows in the Jardin Anglais. If you want to indulge in culture, you can take your pick: contemporary masterpieces at MAMCO, Monet at the Musée d'Art et d'Histoire and opera highs at the Grand Théâtre.

South of the centre, Carouge steals the Little Italy award with its low-slung Piedmont skyline, shady squares and kooky boutiques. A trip to the Left Bank brings you to the boho cafés and funky bars in Plainpalais, while on the Right is Pâquis – a knot of narrow streets where restaurants whip up world flavours and the hip crowd hangs out on the pier. Like all good chocolate boxes, Geneva really does offer something for everyone.

◗ *Statuesque beauty in Mon Repos park*

# When to go

## SEASONS & CLIMATE

Geneva has a temperate climate, but being surrounded by mountains makes it temperamental too – the northerly *bise* wind from the Alps can make it feel chilly and it occasionally snows as late as March and April. However, spring gradually becomes mild, and summers are warm but not too hot, peaking at around 25°C (77°F)

In autumn, expect a final burst of colour in Geneva's parks and the odd shower; it is the ideal time to explore the city's galleries and enjoy leisurely strolls. Winters occasionally bring light snow, with temperatures hovering between 5°C (41°F) and a frosty −2°C (28.4°F). Note that during long holidays such as Christmas and Easter, many shops, restaurants and museums remain closed over the whole period.

## ANNUAL EVENTS
### February & March

**Geneva Carnival** Costumed parades, streams of colourful floats, music, dancing, parties and street entertainment bring carnival fever to Geneva for three days in February or March. ① 078 823 38 21 ⓦ www.carnaval-geneve.ch

**International Motor Show** The city steps up a gear in spring when the motor-mad check out the latest in cars, technology and accessories at this mammoth exhibition held at the Palexpo. ⓐ Palexpo Exhibition Centre ① 022 761 11 11 ⓦ www.salon-auto.ch

## April & May

**AMR Jazz Festival** Jazz, soul and blues rhythms at the Alhambra draw music lovers to Geneva in droves. ⓐ 10 rue des Alpes ⓣ 022 716 56 39 ⓦ www.amr-geneve.ch

**Geneva Marathon** Thousands of runners cover a scenic route through the city. ⓐ Place des Nations ⓣ 022 787 07 53 ⓦ www.genevemarathon.ch

⬤ *Autumnal hues in Parc des Bastions*

## June

**Fête de la Musique** Streets and squares are transformed into open-air stages for this monster music festival, staging everything from chanson to jazz and pop concerts. ☎ 022 418 65 32 Ⓦ www.fetedelamusique.ch

## July & August

**Musiques en Été** From classical concerts to funky jazz, sopranos to African beats, this two-month festival breathes musical life into the city. ☎ 022 418 36 18 Ⓦ www.ville-ge.ch

**Orange Cinema** Catch the latest flicks on a giant, open-air screen at this summer film festival by the lake. Ⓦ www.orangecinema.ch

**Fêtes de Genève** Parades, fireworks and late-night parties make this festival a highlight in Geneva's summer calendar. Best of all, it's free! ☎ 022 909 70 00 Ⓦ www.fetes-de-geneve.ch

## September

**Art'Air** Artists seek inspiration in all corners of the city for this weekend of open-air workshops. ☎ 022 794 89 80 Ⓦ www.artair.ch

**La Bâtie Festival** A celebration of dance, theatre and music across the city. ☎ 022 908 69 50 Ⓦ www.batie.ch

**Fête des Vendanges** Taste the produce of the grape harvest in the nearby village of Russin. As well as free-flowing wine, this intoxicating festival features markets, music and street entertainment. Ⓦ www.russin.ch

## November & December

**Christmas Market** The twinkling market on place de la Fusterie

has stalls with handmade crafts, gingerbread and mulled wine.
ⓐ Place de la Fusterie ❶ Tourist office: 022 909 70 70

**Christmas Ice Rink** Warm up with mulled wine and raclette after a stint on the ice. ⓐ Place du Rhône ❶ Tourist office: 022 909 70 70

**Coup de Noël** A teeth-chattering 125 m (410 ft) swim in Lake Geneva. ⓐ Jardin Anglais ❶ Tourist office: 022 909 70 70

**Festival Arbres & Lumières** Taking place in several locations throughout Geneva, this is a festival celebrating the arrival of the Christmas period with well-known artists decorating Christmas trees with lighting displays, transforming Geneva into a city of spectacular light. ⓦ www.arbresetlumieres.ch

**Fête de l'Escalade** History is revisited at this must-see event celebrating the city's victory in 1602 in riotous fashion (see page 14). ❶ 079 382 92 77 ⓦ www.compagniede1602.ch

---

**PUBLIC HOLIDAYS**
**New Year's Day** 1 Jan
**Good Friday** 2 Apr 2010, 22 Apr 2011, 13 Apr 2012
**Easter Sunday** 4 Apr 2010, 24 Apr 2011, 15 Apr 2012
**Easter Monday** 5 Apr 2010, 25 Apr 2011, 16 Apr 2012
**Ascension Day** 13 May 2010, 2 June 2011, 17 May 2012
**Whit Monday** 24 May 2010, 13 June 2011, 28 May 2012
**Swiss National Day** 1 Aug
**Geneva Fast** 7 Sept
**Christmas Day** 25 Dec
**Restauration Genèvoise** 31 Dec

# Escalade

Fanfare parades, festive revelry and a whole lot of Swiss chocolate smashing make the Escalade the most important event of the year. Held on the weekend closest to 11 December, the unique celebrations commemorate the city's 1602 victory over the Duke of Savoy's troops, who tried to attack Geneva by scaling the city's walls at night. Genevan Catherine Cheynel, better known as the Mère Royaume, stopped some of the attackers dead in their tracks by pouring a pot of scalding vegetable soup over their heads – her determined resistance helped secure Geneva's independence.

The week before the big event, there's a race called the Course de L'Escalade, where hundreds of sprightly locals turn out to stampede through the Old Town's narrow streets to Parc des Bastions – a fun way to keep fit and take in the sights. Many of the runners wear flamboyant costumes.

On the following weekend, festivities build up to Sunday's torchlit parade; this marks the historical event with re-enactments complete with 17th-century costume and artillery demonstrations. As darkness falls, drummers, pipers and trumpeters march past, musketeers on horseback open fire and brave swordsmen display their skills. The noise is ear splitting and the atmosphere electric. The parade winds through the cobbled Old Town to Cathédrale St Pierre, where visitors can warm up with mugs of the infamous vegetable soup and spicy *vin chaud* (mulled wine).

The event culminates with the ritual smashing of the *marmite* (cooking pot). The difference is that today's pots are made of chocolate and filled with marzipan vegetables. The shelves of every *pâtisserie* and *confiserie* in Geneva stock these traditional treats, which should be shattered with a single blow (preferably not over someone's head): a sweet end to an ill-fated invasion.

🔺 *Marzipan vegetables commemorate an ancient victory*

# History

Geneva has seen its fair share of incomers throughout its long and turbulent history, stretching back to 3000 BC when Celtic tribes first settled on the banks of Lake Geneva. The Romans conquered the town in 120 BC and the first written mention of 'Genua' was by Julius Caesar around 52 BC.

The year AD 350 marked a turning point in Geneva's history as Germanic Burgundians occupied the town and bishops took power there, making it their first capital in 443. Less than a century later, Franks stepped in and Geneva became part of the Merovingian Kingdom. In the ninth century, the Burgundian Kingdom retook the reins of power until 1032, when the last King of Burgundy died, at which point the German Empire took over.

Geneva blossomed in the Middle Ages and made its mark on the map with the growing importance of its trade fairs, underpinned by the *combourgeoisie*, an alliance which strengthened the bonds between Geneva, Bern and Fribourg. The Protestant Reformation played a pivotal role in shaping the city and was finally accepted by the people in 1536. Just three years later, one of the key figures in the movement, Jean Calvin, founded the city's college and academy.

At the beginning of the 17th century, attention turned to Savoy, which had for some time posed a threat to Geneva's independence. On the night of 11 December 1602, the Duke of Savoy's troops attempted once again to attack the city by climbing its walls using ladders. But they were driven away by the inhabitants, including the Mère Royaume, who threw a pot of piping hot vegetable soup over attacking soldiers. This is the event that is celebrated at the Escalade (see pages 14–15).

The 18th century spelt a golden age for Geneva, as the watch-making industry and banking sector flourished. Among the city's inhabitants at this time was famous writer and philosopher Jean-Jacques Rousseau, whose writings, proclaiming universal liberty and equality, sowed the seeds of the French Revolution. In 1798, Geneva was annexed to France, but regained its freedom in 1813 after the defeat of Napoleon.

A year after Henry Dunant established the Red Cross in 1863, the Geneva Convention was signed, calling for the protection of victims of war and conflict. These milestones laid the foundations for humanitarian law and explain why Geneva was chosen as the headquarters of the League of Nations in 1919. After World War II, Geneva became established as the European headquarters of the United Nations and boomed economically and socially. Today, Geneva continues to play a fundamental role in world affairs, with its ever-growing crop of international organisations, a prosperous service sector and a high standard of living.

● *The Reformation Wall: figures who shaped the city*

# Lifestyle

Life and style: Geneva has both in abundance, so it's no coincidence that this Swiss city continually ranks high in the yearly Worldwide Quality of Living Survey (usually just behind big brother Zurich at the top of the list). A glance around reveals a clean, safe city with an excellent infrastructure, booming business and a superb range of chic restaurants and bars in which the hard-working

● *Markets are part of Geneva's appealing mix*

residents love to play. You'll instantly feel at home in this welcoming, cosmopolitan city, which is posh but not pretentious, attractive but not overblown, efficient but by no means dull.

The first thing that strikes you is Geneva's relaxed pace of life. With cheery locals that are happy to converse and cars that stop to let you cross the road, this feels a million miles away from the hustle and bustle of most metropolises. This laid-back atmosphere is undoubtedly influenced by the lake, the city's natural escape valve, which is surrounded by beautiful parks and dramatic mountain panoramas. Despite their Rolex watches and passion for champagne, Genevans are well-groomed country kids at heart. With the Alps on their doorstep for skiing in winter and beaches for swimming in summer, it's no wonder they go to work with a spring in their step.

With its mixture of languages and cultures, Geneva is a multi-ethnic melting pot. Genevans tend to have an open-minded attitude and liberal streak. Here, businessmen in smart suits share coffee with penniless poets, while Rastafarians and Portuguese bakers hang out with politicians at the Bains des Pâquis. Beneath the Swiss upper crust lies the world in miniature. Adding a dash of energy to the mix is the lively student population that accounts for the plethora of trendy cafés, ever-evolving art scene and late-night partying in high doses.

The good life is what most people associate with Switzerland and it's certainly true of Geneva, a city that epitomises *joie de vivre*. While locals work hard, they are also experts at enjoying themselves, which is why this grown-up playground is dedicated to every possible pastime – from casinos to wining, shopping to alfresco dining. So relax and savour this extraordinary city.

# Culture

In many senses, Geneva is the cultural heart of Switzerland. No fewer than 30 world-class museums, as well as scores of galleries, theatres, concert halls and live music venues have established this city's international reputation for the arts. And culture here is as much about the present as the past: alive and everywhere. Whenever you visit, there's bound to be something raising the cultural barometer, whether on the stage, screen or canvas, from soulful rhythms at the AMR Jazz Festival to fancy footwork at La Bâtie Festival.

It doesn't matter where you go in Geneva: you can't escape music. If you're seeking classical highs, it has to be place Neuve, home to the Grand Théâtre (the spitting image of Opéra Garnier in Paris), where the acclaimed Orchestre de la Suisse Romande performs, and the rococo-style Victoria Hall where strings and

### ART OF THE ORDINARY

Causing a ripple of excitement in the Swiss art world, Geneva-born artist John M Armleder frequently displays his unique and intriguing work at MAMCO. Art in the ordinary is what his exhibitions are about, bringing together abstract paintings, sculpture, drawings and photos to depict the beauty of the banal. A prime example is furniture art, where tables and chairs are splashed with colour, suggesting that we're not only inspired by art, but also what surrounds it.

◆ *Absorbing culture at the Musée d'Art et d'Histoire*

sopranos raise the roof. At the top of the alternative music tree, innovative venues such as L'Usine, Salle Centrale and Le Chat Noir regularly host jam sessions and concerts from live jazz to world music, techno and rock.

Geneva has more than its fair share of excellent galleries that will satisfy the cravings of art buffs. At the top of the list is the Musée d'Art et d'Histoire, showcasing everything from prehistoric artefacts to masterpieces by Rodin and Konrad Witz. Housed in a former factory, MAMCO is its contemporary contender with its attention-grabbing temporary exhibitions. Other art gems include the Musée Ariana , which covers the entire spectrum of ceramics and glassware, and the Musée Rath, housing an exceptional fine-arts collection. Those that prefer their art outdoors should check out the wacky Schtroumpfs building on the Right Bank, with irregular lines, vivid colours and mosaic patterns that would give Gaudí a run for his money.

The stage has its part to play in Geneva's cultural life, too, with everything from classic to avant-garde productions. For high-quality ballet, opera and theatrical performances, book tickets for the Grand Théâtre or catch cutting-edge drama at the Comédie de Genève. The Théâtre du Grütli is a sound choice for improvised and quirky plays, while Théâtre de Carouge hosts a mix of experimental productions and timeless favourites. L'Usine is the city's darling of the daring and features an adventurous line-up and performances that always cross the boundaries of convention.

▶ *The spires of Cathédrale St Pierre*

# Shopping

Geneva makes no secret of its love for the finer things in life: markets piled high with the freshest produce, *chocolatiers* making mouths water with Swiss truffles and fashion designers showing off the latest trends.

Geneva's shops are open year-round, six days a week. Shopping hours are generally 09.00–19.00 Monday to Saturday, with smaller boutiques often closing for lunch. Major shopping malls and department stores stay open for late-night shopping until 21.00 on Thursdays.

Whether you're determined to shop 'til you drop or simply fancy a bit of window-shopping, every corner of Geneva offers something different. Sniff out the latest styles in the boutiques and high-street stores that pepper the Left Bank. For luxury brands, head for the diamond-encrusted rue du Rhône and rue de la Confédération, where glitzy creations in jewellers like Cartier and Bulgari come with a matching price tag. Carouge is the place to buy one-off crafts, from hand-thrown pots to pralines.

Malls and department stores are also abundant in this shoppers' paradise – something especially welcome in bad weather. Conveniently located near the station, Metro Shopping Cornavin is lined with high-street names like Swarovski, Lacoste and Yves Rocher. Nearby, the six-level Manor department store is the ideal one-stop shop, tempting shoppers to spend on fashion, fragrances and home design. Go to the top floor for panoramic views over Geneva. Slightly more upmarket, Globus on rue du Rhône is well stocked with everything from funky footwear to gourmet flavours in the basement food court.

ACTUELLEMENT
Lait -
cranberry

🔺 *Masses of choice in Geneva's chocolate shops*

## USEFUL SHOPPING PHRASES

**How much is this?**
C'est combien?
*Cey combyahng?*

**Can I try this on?**
Puis-je essayer ceci?
*Pweezh ehssayeh cerssee?*

**My size is...**
Ma taille (clothes)/
ma pointure (shoes) est ...
*Mah tie/mah
pooahngtewr ay ...*

**I'll take this one, thank you**
Je prends celui-ci/
celle-ci, merci
*Zher prahng serlweesi/
sehlsee, mehrsee*

If you're bargain-hunting or looking to fill up your picnic basket, head to one of Geneva's morning markets. Stalls brim with local produce such as fruit, flowers, cheese, honey and handmade breads every Wednesday and Saturday at Carouge's food market (🕐 07.00–14.00). While you're roaming the square, pause to taste freshly baked pastries, drink local wines and soak up the relaxed village atmosphere. On the same days, antique enthusiasts hunt for gems at the Plainpalais Flea Market (🕐 06.30–18.00), crammed with bric-à-brac, musty books, vintage clothes and old vinyl.

It's not hard to find Swiss-made products and quality souvenirs. Multipurpose, classic red Victorinox army knives always make a useful gift. For a lingering taste of Geneva, buy a gift-wrapped box of Zeller's divine truffles or Philippe Pascoët's basil-infused pralines (if they last till you get home...). It wouldn't be Switzerland without Swatch – pick up arty watches at the store on rue du Mont-Blanc.

# Eating & drinking

Geneva excels in the gastro department with hearty fare like cheese fondue and *rösti* on the menu. Dining here doesn't have to be expensive: virtually every restaurant has a good-value *plat du jour* that caters for the budget conscious. So whether you want to reach for the Michelin stars on the quai du Mont-Blanc, eat your way around the world in Pâquis, or snuggle up in a wood-panelled bistro, this city has the place for you.

Do a quick check on your budget and appetite before choosing which area of the city to eat in. Big on character and Swiss staples, the cobbled streets of the Old Town are stacked with cosy brasseries and alpine-style chalets serving dishes such as entrecôte steak and fondue. Many offer good-value lunch specials. Go underground to vaulted cellars where candles flicker, or pull up a chair on the terrace of a *petit bistro* on the place du Bourg de Four for alfresco dining in summer.

For those with a bigger bank balance, the swish restaurants lining the glitzy quai du Mont-Blanc and quai Wilson beckon. This is the place to enjoy haute cuisine, 5-star service and prime views of Lake Geneva. Departing every Thursday and Friday,

**PRICE CATEGORIES**
The restaurant price guides used in this book indicate the approximate cost of a three-course meal for one person, excluding drinks, at the time of writing.
£ up to CHF50   ££ CHF50–100   £££ over CHF100

fondue cruises offer a more affordable slice of luxury on the lake. ⓦ www.cgn.ch

Tired of cheese and chocolate? Head for Pâquis to savour world flavours. This hip corner of Geneva spices things up with everything from feisty Mexican enchiladas to hole-in-the-wall Moroccan oases. With a distinctly multicultural edge, you'll be able to indulge in Lebanese, Thai, Japanese and Portuguese specialities.

Low-key Carouge has plenty of intimate, rustic bistros serving Swiss fare with a Mediterranean twist. Once a Sardinian enclave, the love of all things Italian persists: think antipasti, wood-fired pizza, risotto and fresh fish.

🔺 *Alfresco sustenance on the place du Bourg de Four*

One of the cheapest and most pleasant dining options in summer is an alfresco picnic. Geneva has a string of attractive parks and gardens that are perfect for a picnic when the weather permits. Top choices include the Jardin Anglais and Bain des Pâquis pier, where you can lay your blanket by the lake front and drink in views of the Jet d'Eau fountain, or munch your lunch beside the rhododendrons in the flower-strewn Jardin Botanique. In a city that loves its food, there is no shortage of *pâtisseries, fromageries* and wine shops from which to fill your basket either!

Geneva has plenty of restaurants serving international food, but you mustn't leave without trying the delicious local specialities. Alpine heartiness meets French finesse in Geneva's kitchen, where fresh, locally sourced ingredients are used. Fondue is a perennial favourite and lots of fun – skinny forks are used to dip bread into a bubbling pot of cheese or fruit into thick hot chocolate. Another tasty winter warmer is *rösti* (grated potatoes with onion and bacon). Carnivores should tuck into *longeole* (unsmoked pork sausage flavoured with cumin and fennel) or try *l'assiette valaisanne* (cold meat platter). Other specialities to look out for include lake perch, creamy Tomme cheese and artichoke-like cardoons.

## WALKING ON CHOCOLATE

Chocolate is a firm favourite in Geneva, and every *chocolatier* sells the speciality of the city, *pavés glacés*. The brainchild of the 19th-century confectioner Henri Auer, these creamy chocolates shaped like cobblestones simply melt in your mouth.

Surrounded by vine-clad hills, Geneva is wine country, producing some excellent varieties including crisp Chasselas whites, full-bodied Gamay reds and fruity Pinot Noirs. Those that want to taste the grape where it is grown should make for the wineries in nearby Russin and Satigny.

Tipping is optional in Switzerland. Nearly all restaurants in Geneva include a service charge of 15 per cent, but it's normal to leave a small tip if you were pleased with the service. Locals tend to round off the bill to the nearest few francs or tip between five and ten per cent. In Switzerland, it's standard practice to give the tip direct to the waiter.

## USEFUL DINING PHRASES

**I would like a table for ... people**
Je voudrais une table pour ... personnes
*Zher voodray ewn tabl poor ... pehrson*

**May I have the bill, please?**
L'addition, s'il vous plaît?
*L'adission, seel voo pleh?*

**Waiter/waitress**
Monsieur/Mademoiselle
*M'syer/madmwahzel*

**Does it have meat in it?**
Est-ce que ce plat contient
de la viande?
*Essker ser plah kontyang
der lah veeahngd?*

**Where is the toilet, please?**
Où sont les toilettes,
s'il vous plaît?
*Oo sawng leh twahlet,
seel voo pleh?*

# Entertainment & nightlife

As the sun sets over Mont Blanc, neon lights and twinkling fountains illuminate the lake. While Geneva may not seem wild on the surface, dig deeper and you'll find it has more than enough after-dark action to keep night owls happy. With a lively student population that just wants to have fun, a plethora of ultra-cool lounge bars and underground clubs vying for your attention, this city knows how to let its hair down.

Variety is the spice of this city's nightlife – think divas, dressed up to the nines, sipping cocktails on the quai du Mont Blanc and locals unwinding over a glass of red wine on a terrace in the Old Town; arty types hanging out in Plainpalais bars and fashionistas sharing the dance floor in place de la Fusterie. From grunge to glitz, roulette to reggae, fine wines to perfect pints, Geneva will entertain you.

A night in Geneva begins in typically relaxed fashion with a good meal in one of the Old Town's wood-panelled brasseries and a few drinks on the quai du Mont Blanc. Things pick up around 23.00 as bars lining the Pâquis, Plainpalais and centre fill with high-spirited revellers, and the music is turned up a notch. If you want to shake your booty in one of the hottest clubs in town, don't get there until after midnight.

Geneva's clubbing scene moves from students bopping to urban beats to glamour-pusses sipping champagne as they strut their stuff. Check out the ultra-chic B Club and Platinum Glam Club (you might just get in if you look the part), Café Cuba where partygoers sway to Latino rhythms and 7ème Ciel for house music and Mojitos. One of the most popular clubs for

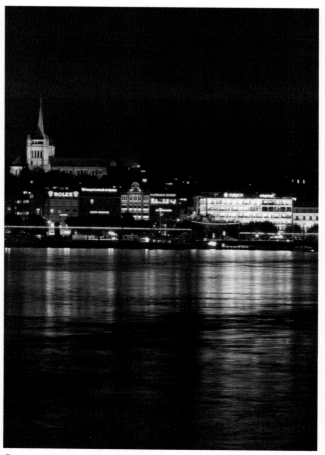

As darkness descends, Geneva lights up

young people and students is **Crem** (ⓐ Boulevard Helvetique 10
ⓣ 022 347 22 20 Ⓦ www.lacrem.ch).

If you're after some more relaxed night-time entertainment,
head to one of Geneva's many pubs and bars. The buzzing place
du Bourg de Four is the place for alfresco drinking and people
watching in summer. For snug British-style pubs with no frills,
a laid-back feel and Guinness on tap, make for the Grand Rue
or rue de Lausanne. The Plainpalais district around rue Bovy-
Lysberg and place du Cirque is the Left Bank's hip heart, serving
up Zen-style lounge bars where the cocktails are creative,
grooves mellow and crowds effortlessly cool.

If you're seeking trendy rather than traditional, you'll
get your kicks in the multicultural Pâquis on the Right Bank.
Clustered here are hole-in-the-wall bars playing everything
from soul to salsa, and the vibe is very much come as you are.
While this is Geneva's red-light district, it's unlikely you'll feel
threatened walking here at night.

Whether you're into sopranos and strings, jazz or comedy the
performing arts are alive and well in Geneva. Classical concerts,
opera and dance raise the roof on the place Neuve, which is
dominated by the acclaimed Grand Théâtre and Conservatoire

## WHAT'S ON
**Geneva Agenda** This online booklet gives up-to-date
listings of events in Geneva. Ⓦ www.geneve-tourisme.ch
**Info Concert** Find the latest festival, concert, theatre and
cinema listings on this French site. Ⓦ www.infoconcert.com

de Musique. For a more offbeat experience, make for funky Le Chat Noir in Carouge, which reels in the crowds with live jazz and jam sessions in the cellar. The Arena is the place for everything from stand-up comedy to musicals and rock concerts.

To book tickets in advance, contact the venue direct or try **Billetnet** (ⓦ www.billetnet.ch), which covers major festivals, gigs and performances.

🔺 *The Grand Théâtre dominates place Neuve*

# Sport & relaxation

## SPECTATOR SPORTS

With a capacity of 30,000, **Stade de Genève** (ⓐ 16 route des Jeunes
ⓣ 022 827 44 00 ⓦ www.servettefc.ch ⓝ Bus: 21, 22 to Stade de
Genève) is home to the city's biggest football club, Servette and
and was a host stadium for the 2008 European Championship.

The multi-purpose arena at Geneva's huge **Palexpo Exhibition
Centre** (ⓐ Grand-Saconnex ⓣ 022 761 11 11 ⓦ www.palexpo.ch
ⓝ Bus: 5, 10, 18 to Palexpo), which is situated next to the airport,
hosts a number of top sporting events including the Showjumping
World Cup.

## PARTICIPATION SPORTS

### Adventure Center

From kayaking the rapids of the Arve River to paragliding from
Mont Salève, this professional centre has 50 years' experience
and offers bags of white-knuckle thrills. There are guides for the
inexperienced or you can hire craft if you prefer to head off on
your own adventure. ⓐ 8 quai des Vernets ⓣ 079 213 41 40
ⓦ www.rafting.ch ⓛ Apr–Oct ⓝ Tram: 15, 17 to Acacias

### Swimming

Geneva has plenty of indoor pools, but when the weather warms,
head for the lake. Make a splash from the Bain des Pâquis pier,
or go to Geneva's beach. **Genève-Plage** (ⓐ Quai de Cologny
ⓣ 022 736 24 82 ⓦ www.geneve-plage.ch ⓛ 10.00–20.00
May–Sept ⓝ Bus: 2, E, G to Genève-Plage. Admission charge)
is set in a large park on the lake edge, and has an Olympic-sized

pool, waterslides, diving boards, volleyball, basketball and children's activities.

## Watersports
The **Wake Sport Centre** (ⓐ 9 quai de Cologny ⓣ 079 202 38 73 ⓦ www.wake.ch ⓛ May–Sept ⓝ Bus: 2, E, G to Genève-Plage) next to Geneva's beach provides waterskiing, wakeboarding, wakeskating and hydrofoiling.

## RELAXATION
### Cruise
**Swissboat** (ⓐ 4–8 quai du Mont-Blanc ⓣ 022 732 47 47 ⓦ www.swissboat.com ⓝ Bus: 29 to Chantepoulet) offer an array of relaxing mini-cruises to take in the sights, as well as trips along the River Rhône.

### Mont Salève
Take the *téléphérique* (cable car) to Geneva's nearest mountain, the 1,380 m (4,527 ft) Mont Salève, where you can hike or mountain bike in summer and cross-country ski in winter. ⓐ Veyrier ⓣ 045 039 86 86 ⓦ www.telepheriquedusaleve.com ⓛ Check website for times ⓝ Bus: 8, 34, 41 to Veyrier-École

### Rousseau Island
Named in honour of philosopher Jean-Jacques Rousseau, this tranquil island in the Rhône is a great place to relax, walk around the bird sanctuary, or enjoy a bite to eat at the island's restaurant with its stunning panoramic views. ⓐ Pont des Bergues ⓦ www.geneve-tourisme.ch

# Accommodation

Swiss hotels are notoriously pricey, but it is also possible to find central hotels that won't break the bank. There's also a good range of character accommodation available in Geneva, including Swiss-chalet, Belle Époque, feng-shui-inspired and boutique-style hotels. The city's hostels offer great value for solo travellers, while campers can enjoy prime lake views.

## HOTELS

**Hôtel Admiral £** This mid-range hotel offers smart rooms decorated in warm hues. Perks include free wireless internet and a hearty breakfast. ⓐ 8 rue Pellegrino Rossi (Right Bank) ⓞ 022 906 97 00 ⓦ www.hoteladmiral.ch Ⓝ Train: Gare Cornavin

**Hôtel Bel'Espérance ££** A central, no-frills hotel. All rooms have satellite TV and the terrace has views over the city's rooftops to Lake Geneva. ⓐ 1 rue de la Vallée (Left Bank) ⓞ 022 818 37 37 ⓦ www.hotel-bel-esperance.ch Ⓝ Tram: 16 to Rive

**Hôtel Bernina ££** Conveniently located opposite the station, this hotel has basic but spotless rooms that won't blow the budget,

### PRICE CATEGORIES
The ratings below indicate the approximate cost of a room for two people for one night in Geneva.
**£** up to CHF150   **££** CHF150–250   **£££** over CHF250

all with cable TV, safe and soundproofed windows. ⓐ 22 place Cornavin (Right Bank) ⓣ 022 908 49 50 ⓦ www.bernina-geneve.ch Ⓝ Train: Gare Cornavin

**Hôtel de la Cloche ££** This intimate, family-run hotel is very central. The 19th-century townhouse has old-world charm with wood floors, a fireplace and cosy rooms – ask for one with a view of the lake. ⓐ 6 Rue de la Cloche (Right Bank) ⓣ 022 732 94 81 ⓦ www.geneva-hotel.ch/cloche Ⓝ Bus: 1 to Monthoux

**Hôtel de Genève ££** A stone's throw from Geneva's key sights, this Belle Époque hotel scores points for its homely feel. The wood-panelled reception recalls an alpine chalet and the rooms are well kept. ⓐ 1 place Isaac-Mercier (Right Bank) ⓣ 022 732 32 64 ⓦ www.hotel-de-geneve.ch Ⓝ Tram: 15, 16 to Isaac-Mercier

**Hôtel des Tourelles ££** Overlooking the Rhône, this charming hotel has attractive, high-ceilinged rooms with soft drapes and hardwood floors. Free Wi-Fi. ⓐ 2 boulevard James-Fazy (Right Bank) ⓣ 022 732 44 23 ⓦ www.destourelles.ch Ⓝ Tram: 13 to Cornavin

**Hôtel Edelweiss £££** Reminiscent of a traditional Swiss chalet, this hotel brings the mountains to the heart of Geneva. The snug rooms have all mod cons including free Wi-Fi access. ⓐ 2 place de la Navigation (Left Bank) ⓣ 022 544 51 51 ⓦ www.manotel.com Ⓝ Bus: 1 to Navigation

**Hôtel Jade £££** Earthy tones create a sense of calm in this feng-shui-inspired hotel near the lake. Free Wi-Fi access. ⓐ 55 rue

◆ *Wallow in luxury at the Hotel Royal*

Rothschild (Left Bank) ☎ 022 544 38 38 ⓦ www.manotel.com
Ⓝ Tram: 13 to Butini

**Hôtel Longemalle £££** With high ceilings, dark wood floors and ornate flourishes, this hotel epitomises Belle Époque elegance. The attractive rooms offer minibar, cable TV and internet access. ⓐ 13 place Longemalle (Left Bank) ☎ 022 818 62 62 ⓦ www.longemalle.ch Ⓝ Bus: 27 to place du Port

**Hôtel Royal £££** Contemporary chic sums up this smart hotel offering 24-hour room service, free wireless internet access and onsite parking. After a long day of sightseeing, unwind in the *hammam* and sauna, or enjoy drinks by the fireside in the lounge. ⓐ 41 rue de Lausanne (Left Bank) ☎ 022 906 14 14 ⓦ www.manotel.com Ⓝ Tram: 13, 15 to Môle

**Hôtel Tiffany £££** This turn-of-the-century boutique hotel is a real find; the plush rooms all have squeaky-clean bathrooms. Relax in the wood-panelled lounge, book a massage and wake up to an excellent breakfast. ⓐ 1 rue des Marbiers (Left Bank) ☎ 022 708 16 16 ⓦ www.hotel-tiffany.ch Ⓝ Tram: 16 to Stand

## HOSTELS
**City Hostel £** Near the main station, this offers single, double and dorm beds. The rooms are clean and there's a communal kitchen, lockers, a TV room and internet access. ⓐ 2 rue Ferrier (Right Bank) ☎ 022 901 15 00 ⓦ www.cityhostel.ch Ⓝ Tram: 13 to Môle

**YH Geneva £** The pick of the budget bunch, this bright and modern hostel has clean and comfortable shared dorms. The good facilities include a laundry, snack bar, internet access and library. Breakfast is included. ⓐ 28–30 rue Rothschild (Left Bank) ⓣ 022 732 62 60 ⓦ www.yh-geneva.ch ⓝ Bus: 1 to Gautier

## CAMPSITES

**Camping Pointe à la Bise £** Enjoy breakfast on the beach at this lakefront site, 10 minutes' drive from Geneva. The camping ground has shady pitches and facilities include a swimming pool, bike hire, restaurant and shop. ⓐ 18 chemin de la Bise, Vésenaz ⓣ 022 752 12 96 ⓦ www.campingtcs.ch ⓛ Mar–Oct ⓝ Bus: E to La Bise

**Camping du Val de l'Allondon £** Situated in a nature reserve, this peaceful campsite is just a short train ride from the centre. ⓐ 106 route de l'Allondon, Satigny ⓣ 022 753 15 15 ⓛ Apr–Oct ⓝ Train: to Satigny

# THE BEST OF GENEVA

There's plenty to enjoy in Geneva, but these are the sights that should really not be missed.

## TOP 10 ATTRACTIONS

- **Cathédrale St Pierre (St Peter's Cathedral)** Scale the North Tower's spiral staircase and see Geneva shrink (see page 60)

- **Bains des Pâquis** Hang out with the hip crowd on the Right Bank's pier (see page 76)

- **MAMCO (Museum of Contemporary Art)** Contemporary art is on the menu at this funky Left Bank gallery (see page 68)

- **Le Chat Noir** The cat's out of the bag – this club is the coolest place in Carouge (see page 101)

- **Jet d'Eau (Water Fountain)** This 140 m (460 ft) fountain rises like a vision above Lake Geneva (see pages 64 & 66)

- **Musée d'Art et d'Histoire (Art & History Museum)** This cavernous museum has everything from paintings by Monet to Egyptian artefacts (see page 68)

- **Horloge Fleurie (Floral Clock)** Created from 6,500 flowers, this celebrates the Swiss tradition of watch- and clock-making (see page 60)

- **Palais des Nations (Palace of Nations)** Take a tour of this political powerhouse (see page 80)

- **Jardin Botanique (Botanical Gardens)** Mediterranean blooms and pink flamingoes vie for attention at these gorgeous lakefront gardens (see page 77)

- **Musée Internationale de la Croix Rouge (International Red Cross Museum)** The work of the world's most famous humanitarian organisation is explored at this fascinating museum (see page 83)

🔽 *The view from the cathedral platform*

# Suggested itineraries

**HALF-DAY: GENEVA IN A HURRY**
Kick off your stay with a whirlwind tour of the hilltop Old Town, winding through narrow streets to take in key sights like the arcaded town hall (see page 64) and turreted Maison Tavel (see page 68). Pause at the medieval Cathédrale St Pierre (see page 60) to climb the North Tower for giddying views over the city's rooftops and lake. Before you leave, be sure to glimpse the flower-strewn Horloge Fleurie and dancing Jet d'Eau from the manicured lawns of the Jardin Anglais (see page 64).

**1 DAY: TIME TO SEE A LITTLE MORE**
A stroll along the lakefront brings you to the vibrant Bains des Pâquis pier (see page 76), where (weather permitting) you can take a quick dip or drink in views of snow-clad Mont Blanc over a coffee. Further along, you'll reach Mon Repos villa and the beautiful Jardin Botanique (see page 77), where pink flamingoes wade. Back on the Left Bank, munch on *rösti* beneath the Taverne de la Madeleine's beams (see page 72), then head for the Musée d'Art et d'Histoire (see page 68) to admire Van Gogh masterpieces and the famous Konrad Witz altarpiece.

**2–3 DAYS: TIME TO SEE MUCH MORE**
Scratch the city's surface to find lesser-known treasures – from cutting-edge exhibitions at MAMCO (see page 68) to the lofty Mur des Réformateurs in the Parc des Bastions (see page 66). After taking a tour of the Palace of Nations (see page 80), pop across to the International Red Cross Museum (see page 83),

which tells a moving tale of triumph and tragedy. Next up, Carouge beckons, with its Sardinian-style houses, pavement cafés and kooky boutiques that are a world away from the buzzing centre. As night falls, catch quirky performances at L'Usine (see page 75) or a live music act at Carouge's Le Chat Noir (see page 101).

## LONGER: ENJOYING GENEVA TO THE FULL

Once you've devoured all Geneva has to offer, get a taste for the surrounding region. Cross the Franco-Swiss border to Annecy (see page 116), where canals flow to the red-turreted medieval castle. Here you can try your hand at mountain climbing or drift away on the lake's translucent waters. Stepping east, enjoy the delights of the Olympic city of Lausanne (see page 104) – from the Gothic heights of Notre-Dame Cathedral via the art gems gracing the walls of the grand Palais de Rumine to the relaxed vibe on the waterfront promenade of Ouchy.

△ Head along the lakefront to buzzing Bains des Pâquis

# Something for nothing

Switzerland has quite a reputation for being expensive, so it's pleasing to discover that some of the best things in Geneva are free. First up is a whirlwind tour of the Old Town that won't cost you a penny (or a Swiss franc, to be precise), where an amble takes in sights such as the arcaded Hôtel de Ville (see page 64), frescoed Tour du Molard (see page 67) and the medieval Cathédrale St Pierre (see page 60) – step inside to admire the magnificent rose window. Wind through narrow cobbled streets to the water's edge, where the Horloge Fleurie (see page 60) keeps ticking and the Jet d'Eau fountain turns heads (see pages 64 & 66).

For a free taste of local life, head for the shady Parc des Bastions (see page 66), where people congregate to play chess on giant boards and the Mur des Réformateurs commemorates key figures of the Reformation. In summer, bring your swimming togs and take a dip from Bains des Pâquis pier (see page 76). This may be a city, but there's plenty of country about: explore Geneva's patchwork of greenery by strolling the Right Bank's promenade. From here you can glimpse sculpture-strewn gardens and gaze at one of the city's most striking sights – the sun setting over Mont Blanc. You can easily spend the afternoon wandering through the vast Jardin Botanique (see page 77), home to cactuses, fragrant plants and deer.

If all that exercise has made you thirsty, be sure to pick up a leaflet from the tourist office giving a comprehensive list of wineries offering free tastings every Saturday. For the cost of a bus ticket, you could vine-hop your way around the winegrowing villages of Anières, Céligny, Russin and Satigny. It costs nothing to get your cultural fix in many of Geneva's intoxicating galleries and museums. Art buffs should make a beeline for the Musée d'Art et d'Histoire (see page 68) to brush up against Rembrandts and Roman treasures, or the sublime Musée Ariana (see page 82) to gawp at precious porcelain. Savvy travellers time their visit to coincide with the first Sunday of the month, when most museums are free, including the must-see MAMCO (see page 68) and Musée Rath (see page 69).

◯ *Musée Ariana: see the ceramic collection for free*

# When it rains

When the rain comes, Geneva shines, with a host of indoor activities to help you forget about the wet weather. If you feel like hibernating, the Old Town has a glut of cosy cafés and low-beamed bistros that are just the ticket. And no country does comfort food like the Swiss – everything seems much brighter over a mug of real hot chocolate or a *caquelon* (a type of pot) filled with cheese fondue to warm your cockles. When the heavens open, the arty cafés around Plainpalais are a great place to hang out with a bottomless cup of coffee and a good book.

Undercover shopping can be the ultimate pick-me-up when it rains. To escape sudden showers, scoot into Globus (see page 70) on rue du Rhône to immerse yourself in the latest styles and tasty specialities in the basement food court. A stone's throw from Carouge, modern **La Praille** mall (❶ 022 304 80 00 Ⓦ www.la-praille.ch) shelters 80 high-street shops selling everything from prune juice to pralines, plus tea rooms, restaurants and a bowling alley.

Culture can compensate for dull skies, too. Go down instead of up at the cathedral to view centuries-old foundations at the archaeological site (see page 60). A few paces away, the medieval Maison Tavel (see page 68) traces Geneva's history with elaborate art and artefacts. Immerse yourself in contemporary creations at MAMCO (see page 68), then pop over to the elegant Musée Patek Philippe (see page 69) to gawp at art nouveau timepieces. Escape heavy downpours at the heartrending Musée Internationale de la Croix Rouge (see page 83) to learn more about the humanitarian work of this international organisation.

It may be too nippy for a dip in the lake, but that's all the more excuse to test out the state-of-the-art *hammam* and sauna complex at the Bain des Pâquis (see page 76). A long steam in the Turkish bath or a soothing massage will leave you feeling as fresh as a daisy. If you've got cash to splash, the ultimate boost on a drizzly day is a trip to the exclusive La Réserve spa (see page 84), which has a huge range of feel-good therapies to chase away rainy-day blues.

🔺 *A temple to timekeeping*

# On arrival

## TIME DIFFERENCE

Switzerland runs on Central European Time (CET), which is an hour ahead of Greenwich Mean Time (GMT). Daylight saving applies: clocks are put forward one hour at the end of March and back one hour at the end of October, on the same day as in the UK.

## ARRIVING

### By air

A major international hub, **Aéroport Genève-Cointrin** (**☎** 022 717 71 11 **ⓦ** www.gva.ch) is 5 km (3 miles) from the centre. See page 128 for details of airlines that operate from the airport.

The modern airport offers an excellent range of facilities open seven days a week, including shops, cafés, ATMs, car hire, a post office, bureau de change, supermarket and pharmacy.

A train shuttles passengers between the airport and Geneva's main station in just eight minutes (trains depart every ten minutes). Alternatively you can take bus number 10 into town, which departs every ten minutes. The Unireso information desk in the arrivals hall provides tickets and details on routes and timetables.

A taxi to the centre will set you back about 80–100 Swiss francs.

### By rail

**Swiss Federal Railways** (**☎** 0900 300 300 **ⓦ** www.sbb.ch) are renowned for their efficiency and comfort, and operate a regular service to Swiss cities including Lausanne (45 minutes), Bern

**IF YOU GET LOST, TRY …**

**Do you speak English?**
Parlez-vous anglais?
*Pahrlay-voo ahnglay?*

**Is this the way to…?**
C'est la bonne direction pour…?
*Seh lah bon deerekseeawng poor…?*

**Can you point to it on my map?**
Pouvez-vous me le montrer sur la carte?
*Poovehvoo mer ler mawngtreh sewr lah kart?*

(two hours) and Zurich (three hours); in addition to French destinations like Lyon (two hours) and Paris (three hours).

The main train station, **Gare Cornavin** (ⓐ Place Cornavin ⓣ 0900 300 300 ⓦ www.cff.ch), is located on the Right Bank and has a good range of facilities including left luggage, a bureau de change and a post office.

### By road

Long-distance buses and international coaches arrive at the city's central bus station, **Gare Routière** (ⓐ Place Dorcière ⓣ 022 732 02 30 ⓦ www.gareroutiere.ch). For information on coach excursions and bus transfers to French ski resorts, see ⓦ www.geneva.ch/f/GenevaCoachStation.htm

Geneva is well connected to the rest of Switzerland and Europe via the A40 (L'Autoroute Blanche) to the French Alps, the A42 to Lyon, and the A1 to Lausanne. For the centre, follow the signs for Genève-Lac and the route de Lausanne. Although driving in Geneva is relatively hassle-free compared to other

major cities, parking can be expensive and difficult to find. Plan in advance by checking the location of multi-storey and Park & Ride car parks on Ⓦ www.geneve.ch. The speed limit is strictly observed in Switzerland and you should display a *Vignette* (toll sticker) in the windscreen at all times

## FINDING YOUR FEET

You will soon feel at home in Geneva, a cosmopolitan city with a laid-back feel and a pedestrianised Old Town. Many locals are fluent in English and happy to direct travellers.

As Geneva is a safe city with a low crime rate, it's unlikely you'll experience any problems during your stay, but it's always wise to keep an eye on your valuables and be careful if walking through dimly lit, less-populated areas at night.

● *The action in Geneva centres around the lake*

**OLD TOWN TOURS**

Jump aboard a traditional road train for a tour around the Old Town. The 40-minute tour covers Geneva University, Cathédrale St Pierre, and La Statue Pictet de Rochemont, with guides explaining the history behind the sights. Other tours offered include a panoramic trip around the hills of Geneva to see the Jet d'Eau, Floral Clock, Grange Park, and Brunswick Monument. Tours depart from place du Rhône and quai du Mont Blanc. **STT Trains Tours** ☏ 022 781 04 04 ⓦ www.sttr.ch

## ORIENTATION

Hemmed in by the Alps and straddling the Franco-Swiss border, Geneva is located in Switzerland's southwest corner. Split in two by the snaking River Rhône, the city hugs the banks of Lake Geneva and is framed by mountains.

Most of the action centres around the lake: the UN institutions, Jardin Botanique and Les Pâquis on the Right Bank and Cathédrale St Pierre, the Jet d'Eau fountain and the Plainpalais on the Left. Carouge is just south of the centre.

## GETTING AROUND

Geneva's efficient public transport network makes it simple to get around. If you're making several trips, it's worth picking up a 48- or 72-hour Geneva Transport Card from the tourist office for unlimited use of the city's trams, buses, boats and trains.

Trams are one of the fastest and most reliable ways to get

about the city. Geneva's six tram lines crisscross the city and operate from 06.00 to 00.00. Each stop has a ticket machine, for which you'll need exact change. Geneva's dependable bus network also operates from 06.00 to 00.00 with a night service at weekends. You'll find bus and tram route maps and timetables at each stop. Alternatively, call ⓣ 0900 022 021 or see ⓦ www.tpg.ch

Geneva encourages pedal power, and from May to October bikes can be borrowed for free. For details, contact **Genève Roule** (ⓣ 022 740 13 43 ⓦ www.geneveroule.ch).

With so much water, it's often convenient to get around Geneva by boat. Pick a cruise or simply hop aboard one of the yellow-and-white ferries (*mouettes*) that shuttle passengers every ten minutes between Pâquis, Eaux-Vives and Place du Molard. Information is available on ⓦ www.swissboat.com

## CAR HIRE
Geneva's excellent public transport network means you can get around easily. However, if you're planning on going further afield, hiring a car could be a good option. All of the following car hire companies have outlets at the airport.

**Avis** Also at: ⓐ 44 rue de Lausanne ⓣ 022 731 90 00 ⓦ www.avis.com

**Budget** ⓣ 022 717 86 75 ⓦ www.budget.com

**Europcar** ⓣ 022 717 81 10 ⓦ www.europcar.com

**Hertz** ⓣ 022 717 80 80 ⓦ www.hertz.com

ⓓ *Committed to peace: a statue near the Palais des Nations*

# Left Bank

If you're looking for variety, Geneva's Left Bank will not disappoint: from the medieval Old Town in the shadow of the cathedral spires to the glittering lakefront where the Floral Clock ticks and the Plainpalais and its ultra-cool bars. Whether you want to chill in shady parks, wallow in modern art, gorge on fondue or boutique-shop along Grand Rue, you can graze for days on the Left Bank's riches.

## SIGHTS & ATTRACTIONS

### Cathédrale St Pierre (St Peter's Cathedral)

The medieval monolith rises like a vision above Geneva's Old Town. The edifice is a fusion of Romanesque, Gothic and neoclassical styles – step inside to admire its cross-ribbed vaulting and huge rose window. Underground is an archaeological site that traces the cathedral's early foundations. But if you're seeking highs, climb the North Tower's steep spiral staircase to view the bell tower and spires. The terrace affords bird's-eye views over the city's rooftops, lake and mountains. ⓐ Place St. Pierre ⓣ 022 319 71 91 ⓦ www.saintpierre-geneve.ch ⓛ 09.30–18.30 Mon–Sat, 12.30–18.30 Sun, June–Sept; 10.00–12.00, 14.00–17.00 Mon–Fri, 10.00–17.30 Sat, 12.00–17.30 Sun, Oct–May ⓝ Bus: 36 to Cathédrale. Admission charge (North Tower)

### Horloge Fleurie (Floral Clock)

A living tribute to a country that runs like clockwork, this blooming beautiful clock in the Jardin Anglais will have you reaching for

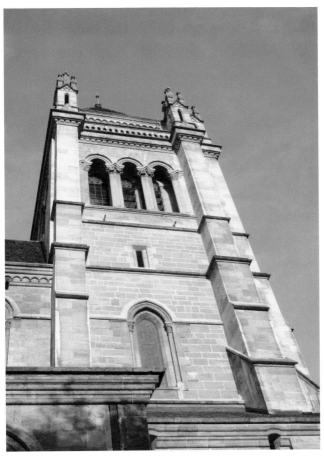

◆ *Reach the dizzy heights at Cathédrale St Pierre*

**Left Bank**

| 0 | 200 metres |
| 0 | 200 yards |

N

RUE DU GEVRAY

RUE DU LÉMAN

PLACE JEAN-MARTEAU

QUAI DU MONT-BLANC

RUE PH. PLANTAMOUR

Jetée des Pâquis

Bains des Pâquis

*Lake Geneva*

Jetée des Eaux-Vives

Jet d'Eau

FRONTENEX

Parc la Grange

PROMENADE DU LAC

QUAI GUSTAVE-ADOR

Horloge Fleurie
Jardin Anglais

MARIE D'ALIBACKE

RUE DU SIMPLON

RUE DALLÉMAN

RUE DU LAC

RUE D'ITALIE

RUE DE DAVIENE

PIERRES DU LION DE LA MARE

R. G-MUSSY

RUE SCIE

RUE VERSONNEX

RUE DU RHÔNE

ÉTIENNE AOSTE

RUE D'ITALIE AOSTE

AVENUE WILLIAM FAVRE

RUE EAUX-VIVES

RUE DES VOLLANDES

AVENUE E. HENTSCH

RUE BLANVALET

RUE DU BL

RUE DE MONTCHOISY

RUE DU NANT

LEFT BANK

AVENUE E. PICTET-DE-ROCHEMONT

ROND-POINT DE RIVE

BOULEVARD HELVÉTIQUE

AVE DE FRONTENEX

AVENUE PICTET-DE-ROCHEMONT

ROUTE DE FRONTENEX

9 DÉCEMBRE

HELVÉTIQUE

RUE P. JAULIAN

RUE FRÉD MULLER

GLACIS DE RIVE

RUE ADR-LACHENAL

RUE DE LA TERRASSIÈRE

RUE DE VILLEREUSE

AVE DE CHAMONIX

CHÊNE-BOUGERIES

ROUTE DE CHÊNE

RUE P. POPPLER

RUE DE ROCHES

CH. DE ROCHES

AVENUE TH. WEBER

RUE AGASSE

CH. CLOS-BELMONT

AVE DE LAMANDOLIER

CHARLES-GALLAND

Parc de Malagnou

RUE TR-CRAST

BOULEVARD DES TRANCHÉES

RUE DE BEAUMONT

ROUTE DE MALAGNOU

RUE DE CONTAMINES

R. T. MUSSARD

your camera. Around 6,500 brightly coloured flowers and plants
are used to create new displays each spring and autumn to celebrate
Switzerland's famous watch-making industry. ⓐ Jardin Anglais,
quai du Général-Guisan Ⓝ Bus: 27 to place du Port

### Hôtel de Ville (Town Hall)

With its arcades overlooking a cobbled inner courtyard, Geneva's
town hall has been the cogs and wheels of the city's political
life since the 15th century and is still the seat of the cantonal
government. Just opposite, take a peek at the Old Arsenal,
a former granary with impressive canons and mosaic frescoes
depicting historical scenes. ⓐ Rue de l'Hôtel-de-Ville Ⓛ 08.00–12.30,
13.30–17.30 Mon–Sat Ⓝ Bus: 36 to Hôtel de Ville

### Jardin Anglais (English Garden)

This ever-so-English garden is laced with paths that pass
dancing fountains, statues and a bandstand. Find a shady spot
beneath the oak trees, take a cruise on the lake or wander along

### WATERWORKS

Now the focal point of the lake, Geneva's famous Jet d'Eau
was originally just a security valve. Over the years the
locals grew quite attached to this huge fountain – one of
the largest in the world. Today it shoots around 500 litres
(132 gallons) of water per second into the sky and, when
the sun shines, creates a rainbow that can best be admired
from the Pont du Mont Blanc bridge.

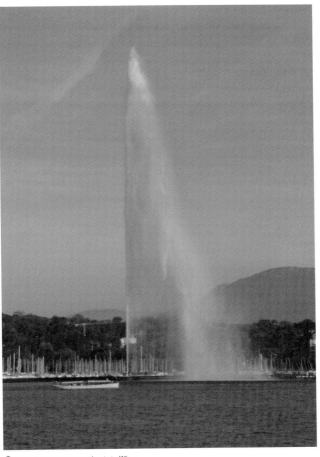

� Splashing success: the Jet d'Eau

## CULTURE

### Grand Théâtre (Opera House)

Dominating place Neuve, this grand 19th-century opera house has earned an international reputation for its world-class opera, theatre, ballet and recitals. The season runs from October to May. ⓐ 11 boulevard du Théâtre ⓣ 022 418 30 00 ⓦ www.geneveopera.ch ⓝ Tram: 12, 17 to place Neuve

### Maison Tavel

Set in the city's oldest medieval residence, this fascinating museum features displays of antique furniture, tapestries and silverware spanning the Middle Ages to the 20th century. Be sure to look at the model of pre-1850 Geneva. ⓐ 6 rue du Puits St Pierre ⓣ 022 418 37 00 ⓦ www.ville-ge.ch ⓛ 10.00–17.00 Tues–Sun ⓝ Tram: 16 to Molard. Admission charge for temporary exhibitions

### MAMCO (Museum of Contemporary Art)

This former factory is now the driving force behind Geneva's contemporary art scene, presenting fresh and edgy temporary exhibitions that focus on artists like John M Armleder and a broad variety of mediums. ⓐ 10 rue des Vieux-Grenadiers ⓣ 022 320 61 22 ⓦ www.ville-ge.ch/mah ⓛ 12.00–18.00 Tues–Fri, 11.00–18.00 Sat & Sun ⓝ Bus: 1 to École-Médecine. Admission charge

### Musée d'Art et d'Histoire (Art & History Museum)

A must-see for culture vultures, this cavernous museum covers fine arts, archaeology and applied arts, presenting everything from Egyptian antiquities to Roman pottery and medieval weaponry. Art lovers should head straight for the permanent collection of masterpieces from the likes of Rembrandt, Monet and Van Gogh. A highlight is Konrad Witz's 15th-century altarpiece. ⓐ 2 rue Charles-Galland ⓣ 022 418 26 00 ⓦ www.ville-ge.ch/mah ⓛ 10.00–17.00 Tues–Sun ⓝ Bus: 1, 7 to Rive

## Musée Patek Philippe (Patek Philippe Museum)

A temple to Swiss timekeeping, this opulent museum shelters a peerless collection of antique and Patek Philippe timepieces, from elaborate 17th-century pocket watches to art nouveau pendant designs and astronomical clocks. ⓐ 7 rue des Vieux-Grenadiers ⓣ 022 807 09 10 ⓦ www.patekmuseum.com ⓛ 14.00–18.00 Tues–Fri, 10.00–18.00 Sat ⓝ Bus: 1 to École-Médecine. Admission charge

## Musée Rath (Rath Museum)

Housed in a neoclassical building, this fine arts museum showcases the collection of 19th-century benefactor Simon Rath and frequently stages first-rate exhibitions. ⓐ 2 place Neuve ⓣ 022 418 33 40 ⓛ 10.00–17.00 Tues, Thur–Sun, 12.00–21.00 Wed ⓝ Tram: 12, 17 to place Neuve. Admission charge ⓘ Closed for renovation until winter 2009

## Salle Centrale

If you're seeking an alternative cultural scene, this venue screening art-house films and staging experimental productions could be just the ticket. The centre's eclectic programme stretches from flamenco to concerts, exhibitions to improvised plays. ⓐ 10 rue de la Madeleine ⓣ 079 397 25 40 ⓦ www.sallecentrale.ch ⓝ Tram: 12, 16

## RETAIL THERAPY

**Boulevard du Vin** Sniff out Pinots and Sauvignon Blancs at this sleek cellar where you can taste the wines before you buy. ⓐ 1–3 boulevard Georges-Favon ① 022 310 91 90 ⓦ www.boulevard-du-vin.ch ① Shop: 10.00–19.00 Mon–Fri, 10.00–17.00 Sat, 16.00–19.00 Sun; Bar: 16.00–23.00 Mon–Fri ⓝ Tram: 15 to Stand

**Globus** On the main shopping drag, this smart five-level department store has everything a shopaholic could desire: from fashion to sportswear, cosmetics and a glorious food court. ⓐ 48 rue du Rhône ① 022 319 50 50 ⓦ www.globus.ch ① 09.00–19.00 Mon–Wed, 09.00–21.00 Thur, 09.00–19.30 Fri, 09.00–18.00 Sat ⓝ Tram: 16 to Molard

**Luci Mendola** Handcrafted bangles, strings of beads and unusual rings fill this chic boutique. ⓐ 16 rue Verdaine ① 022 310 05 93 ⓦ www.luci-mendola.com ① 14.00–18.30 Mon, 10.00–18.30 Tues, Thur & Fri, 11.00–18.30 Wed, 10.00–17.00 Sat ⓝ Bus: 27 to place du Port

**Plainpalais Flea Market** Eagle-eyed bargain hunters spend the morning rummaging through antiques, vintage clothes, old records, books and bric-à-brac at this atmospheric flea market. ⓐ Plaine de Plainpalais ① 022 418 83 00 ① 06.30–18.00 Wed & Sat ⓝ Tram: 12, 13 to Rond-Point de Plainpalais

**Theodora** Romance, nostalgia and the scent of lavender drift from this perfumer par excellence, where you'll find signature fragrances like Rosine rose perfumes and Santa Maria Novella eaux de toilette. ⓐ 38 Grand Rue ⓣ 022 310 38 75 ⓦ www.parfumerietheodora.ch ⓛ 09.30–18.30 Tues, Wed & Fri, 09.30–19.00 Thur, 09.30–17.30 Sat

**Zeller** This dreamy *chocolatier* has a glass counter full of exquisite pralines, truffles, marzipan creations and melt-in-your-mouth *pavés glacés* (cobblestone-shaped chocolates). It's a secret too sweet to keep... ⓐ 1 place de Longemalle ⓣ 022 311 50 26 ⓛ 08.00–18.45 Mon–Fri, 08.00–18.00 Sat ⓝ Bus: 8, 27 to place du Port

## TAKING A BREAK

**Alhambar £** ❶ Red velvet armchairs, art deco lamps and spacey lighting make this a top choice for Sunday brunch, fresh salads or filling pasta dishes. By night, the vintage-style café becomes a lively bar attracting a cool crowd. ⓐ 10 rue de la Rôtisserie ⓣ 022 312 13 13 ⓦ www.alhambar.com ⓛ 12.00–14.00 Mon, 12.00–14.00, 17.00–01.00 Tues & Wed, 12.00–14.00, 17.00–02.00 Thur & Fri, 16.00–02.00 Sat, 11.00–00.00 Sun ⓝ Tram: 16 to Molard

**Le Rozzel £** ❷ Hobbit-like windows and a tiny terrace add to the appeal of this crêperie in the Old Town, where you can satisfy your pancake cravings with sweet and savoury varieties. ⓐ 18 Grand Rue ⓣ 022 311 89 29 ⓛ 11.00–18.00 Mon–Sat ⓝ Tram: 16 to Molard

**Taverne de la Madeleine £ ❸** For local flavour and great-value lunches, make for this centuries-old tavern with creaking beams, exposed stone and the hum of chatter. Homemade fare includes dishes like *rösti* potatoes and pike-perch filet. ⓐ 20 rue Toutes-Âmes, off place de la Madeleine ⓣ 022 310 60 70 ⓛ 07.30–18.30 Mon–Fri (last orders 16.00), 09.00–16.30 Sat (last orders 14.30), Sept–June; 07.30–21.00 Tues–Sat (last orders 20.00), July & Aug ⓝ Bus: 8, 27 to place du Port

## AFTER DARK

### RESTAURANTS
**Chez ma Cousine 'on y mange du poulet' £ ❹** Spit-roasted chicken served with mounds of Provençal potatoes is the reason to visit this rustic, good-value restaurant in the centre of town. ⓐ 6 place du Bourg-de-Four ⓦ www.chezmacousine.ch ⓛ 11.30–23.30 ⓝ Bus: 3, 5 to Croix-Rouge

**Le Morgan £ ❺** Low ceilings and wood panelling give this vaulted cellar a cave-like feel. Take a pew to enjoy classic bistro fare in a warm, friendly setting. ⓐ 14 rue de la Madeleine ⓣ 022 311 81 00 ⓛ 11.30–14.30, 17.00–21.00 Mon–Fri ⓝ Bus: 8, 27 to place du Port

**Brasserie de l'Hôtel de Ville ££ ❻** There is an old-world feel about this bistro with its polished brass and antique-lined walls. The fare is Swiss with favourites like Geneva-style pork and fondue on the menu. The terrace comes alive in summer. ⓐ 39 Grand Rue ⓣ 022 311 70 30 ⓔ glosu@bluewin.ch ⓛ 07.00–23.00 Mon–Fri, 10.00–23.00 Sat & Sun ⓝ Bus: 3, 5 to Croix-Rouge

**Café des Bains ££** ❼ Near the MAMCO, this modern restaurant dishes up poetry on a plate: think sautéed gambas with prune chutney and polenta or Kerala curry with cumin-glazed carrots. ⓐ 26 rue des Bains ⓣ 022 321 57 98 ⓦ www.cafedesbains.com ⓛ 11.00–15.00, 18.00–01.00 Tues–Sat ⓝ Bus: 1 to École-Médecine

**Café Papon ££** ❽ Dine beneath the vaults at this chic restaurant near the Parc des Bastions. Foodies come to mingle and enjoy tender veal and morels in cream sauce and a nice glass of wine. ⓐ 1 rue Henri-Fazy ⓣ 022 311 54 28 ⓦ www.cafe-papon.com ⓛ 07.00–23.00 Mon–Fri, 09.30–23.00 Sat ⓝ Bus: 3, 5 to Croix-Rouge

**Au Pied de Cochon ££** ❾ Pig's trotters are the speciality of this ever-popular brasserie oozing turn-of-the-century charm. Service here is snappy and the food delicious. ⓐ 4 place du Bourg-de-Four ⓣ 022 310 47 97 ⓦ www.pied-de-cochon.ch ⓛ 06.00–23.00 Mon–Fri, 09.00–23.00 Sat & Sun ⓝ Bus: 3, 5 to Croix-Rouge

**Senso ££** ❿ Clean lines, muted tones and brown leather create an ultra-modern setting in which to feast on Italian fusion cuisine. Olive trees provide shade in the inner courtyard. ⓐ 56 rue du Rhône ⓣ 022 310 39 90 ⓦ www.senso-living.ch ⓛ 12.00–15.00, 17.00–02.00 Mon–Sat ⓝ Bus: 29 to Molard

**U Bobba Restaurant ££** ⓫ This restaurant celebrates Emilio Bobba, a poet with a passion for gourmet food. The restaurant is sophisticated but affordable. ⓐ 21 rue de la Corraterie ⓣ 022 310 53 40 ⓛ 11.30–15.00, 18.30–00.30 Mon–Thur, 11.30–15.00, 18.30–01.30 Fri & Sat ⓝ Bus: 3 to Bovy-Lysberg

## BARS & CLUBS

**7ème Ciel** With moody lighting and sleek contours, this relaxed lounge bar draws trendy urbanites that come to sip mojitos as DJs spin oriental and house tunes. The décor and people are beautiful. ⓐ 7 rue de la Corraterie ⓣ 022 810 12 40 ⓛ 17.00–02.00 Mon–Sat ⓝ Bus: 3 to Bovy-Lysberg

**BBM Wine Bar** A red cow welcomes you to this great little wine bar. Decked out with funky light bulbs and black leather walls, it also has a terrace with lake views and is great for an aperitif. ⓐ Quai du Général-Guisan ⓣ 022 310 92 36 ⓔ bbmwinebar@hotmail.com ⓛ 12.00–15.00, 17.00–02.00 Mon–Sat ⓝ Bus: 1, 10 to Bel-Air

**B Club** Bright young things dress up to the nines and head for this über-cool club to dance till the sun rises. You may well be sharing the dance floor with celebrities... ⓐ 12 place de la Fusterie ⓣ 022 311 05 55 ⓦ www.lebaroque.ch ⓛ 23.30–05.00 Mon, Tues & Thur–Sat, 19.00–05.00 Wed ⓝ Bus: 1, 10 to Bel-Air

**Café Cuba** Latino grooves and salsa moves make this a top after-dark choice. The crowd is hip, the vibe chilled and the caipirinhas flow freely. ⓐ 1 place du Cirque ⓣ 022 328 44 52 ⓦ www.cafecuba.ch ⓛ 19.00–01.00 or 02.00 Mon–Fri, 17.00–02.00 Sat ⓝ Tram: 15 to Cirque

**Demi Lune Café** Fashionable but understated, candles flicker and mellow grooves play at this cosy bar, where you can sink into a sofa and munch tapas with your cocktail. ⓐ 3 rue Etienne-Dumont

☎ 022 312 12 90 🌐 www.demilune.ch 🕙 10.00–01.00 Mon–Wed,
10.00–02.00 Thur & Fri, 16.00–02.00 Sat, 16.00–01.00 Sun
Ⓝ Bus: 3, 5 to Croix-Rouge

**L'Ethno Bar** Go boho in this arty bar and gallery with high
ceilings, wood floors and pillar-box red walls. Everyone who's
anyone comes here: students to write, musicians to compose
and eco-warriors to plot how to save the world. By night, the
ambience is upbeat. 🄰 1 rue Bovy-Lysberg ☎ 023 310 25 21
🌐 www.ethnobar.ch 🕙 07.00–02.00 Mon–Fri, 10.00–02.00
Sat & Sun Ⓝ Tram: 15 to Cirque

**Spring Brothers** A laid-back pub in the centre of town with
Guinness on tap and big-screen sports. 🄰 23 Grand Rue
☎ 022 312 40 08 🕙 17.00–02.00 Ⓝ Bus: 3, 5 to place Neuve

**L'Usine** Urban beats pump out from this trendy venue for
alternative arts, housed in a former factory. The superb line-up
moves from concerts to cutting-edge plays, films and club nights.
🄰 4 place des Volontaires ☎ 022 781 34 90 🌐 www.usine.ch
🕙 12.00–15.00, 17.00–02.00 Mon–Sat Ⓝ Bus: 10 to Palladium

# Right Bank

Five-star hotels punctuating the quai du Mont-Blanc, crystalline high-rises around the Palace of Nations, boho chic in multicultural Pâquis and gardens hugging the banks of Lake Geneva – the Right Bank has all of this and more. Whether you're seeking the best views of snow-white Mont Blanc, the shade of giant sequoias, a soak in a luxury spa or a mean curry, this district can provide it.

The beauty of the Right Bank lies in its contradictions: from politicians on UN business to Brazilian bartenders in the up-and-coming Pâquis, all-night partying in the Platinum Glam Club to the peace of Mon Repos park.

## SIGHTS & ATTRACTIONS

### Bains des Pâquis

With seagulls soaring above, waves lapping against the shore and a lighthouse, this pier in central Geneva wouldn't look out of place at the seaside. This wooden boardwalk is where locals gather for a stroll, coffee or picnic – from sharply dressed business people to students relaxing on the rocks. If you're seeking Geneva's hip side, look no further. It also has beaches from which you can swim – even in winter if you want to give the plucky Genevans a run for their money. There's also a sauna and *hammam* where you can warm up after the big chill. ⓐ 30 quai du Mont-Blanc ⓘ 022 732 29 74 ⓦ www.bains-des-paquis.ch ⓛ 10.00–21.30 ⓝ Bus: 1 to Pâquis

## Brunswick Monument

The architectural equivalent of a wedding cake, this ornate pink-and-white monument is a riot of skinny spires and stone latticework. The mausoleum is the final resting place of eccentric Duke Charles II of Brunswick, who left his entire fortune to Geneva. Frivolous but fun. ⓐ Quai du Mont-Blanc ⓝ Bus: 1 to Monthoux

## Jardin Botanique (Botanical Gardens)

You can spend an entire afternoon roaming the city's botanical gardens, which fringe the banks of Lake Geneva. The vast green space features an arboretum, Mediterranean greenhouse and gardens nurturing herbs, vegetables, vines, medicinal plants, magnolias and rhododendrons. There are hands-on displays

⬤ The lighthouse at Bains des Pâquis

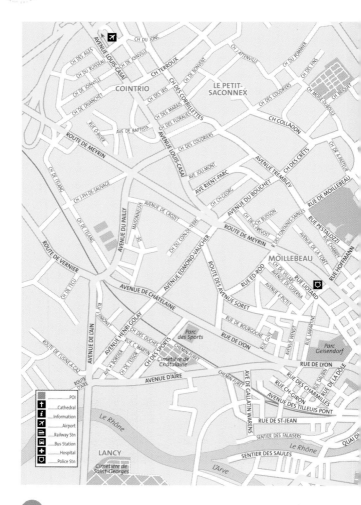

CH DU JONC
CH DE LATTENVILLE
CH DU BONMIER
AVENUE LOUIS-CASAÏ
CH DES AILES
CH DU RUISSEAU
CH DE JOINVILLE
CH TERROUX
CH DE BONVENT
CH DES COUDRIERS
CH DES FINS
CH MON-IDÉE
CH BRIQUET
COINTRIO
CH DES IRIS
CH DES CORBILLETTES
LE PETIT-SACONNEX
CH DE JOINVILLE
CH DE DIVONCHET
CH DES MARAIS
CH COLLADON
RUE CRIDOR
CH DES FLORALIES
CH DE L'ASTEUR
AVE DE BAPTISTA
AVENUE TREMBLEY
CH DES CRETS
ROUTE DE MEYRIN
AVENUE LOUIS-CASAÏ
CH DES COUDRIERS
RUE DE MOILLEBEAU
CH DE TÉLANG
AVE JOLIMONY
AVENUE DU BOUCHET
CH DU BUISSON
RUE PESTALOZZI
CH J.PH.DE SAUVAGE
AVE RIENT-PARC
CH CH.-GEORG
CHS-FONTAINES-SAINTES
AVENUE DE LA FORÊT
CH CHABRY
AVENUE DE CROZET
ROUTE DE MEYRIN
RUE HOFFMANN
CH DE TÉLANG
AVENUE DU PAILLY
MAISONNETTE
CH DU CONCHE-TERRE
MOILLEBEAU
ROUTE DE VERNIER
DE
CH DE VILLARD
RUE ED.-ROD
RUE LIOTARD
CH DE TÉCU
AVENUE EDMOND-VAUCHER
ROUTE DES AVENUE SORET
AVENUE E.-PICTET
AVENUE E.-TUFERNA
AVENUE DE CHÂTELAINE
RUE DE BOURGOGNE
RUE CUIE
RUE HENRI
AVENUE DE L'AIN
PITIT
SIMONET
AVENUE HENRI GOLAY
CH DES DUCHES
RUE DE LYON
AVENUE HENRI
RUE LAMARTINE
ROUTE DE L'USINE-À-GAZ
AVE H.BORDIER
RUE C MARTIN
CH DES SPORTS
Parc des Sports
CHEMIN FURET
Parc Geisendorf
AVE DE TESSOR
Cimetière de Châtelaine
RUE DE LYON
ROUTE D'AIRE
AVENUE D'AIRE
CHEMIN FURET
AVE DE GALLATIN WARENS
RUE DES CHARMILLES
RUE DALBIN
RUE DE LA DÔLE
AVE CH.-GIRON
AVENUE DES TILLEULS PONT
Le Rhône
RUE DE ST-JEAN
QUAI DU
SENTIER DES FALAISES
Le Rhône
LANCY
SENTIER DES SAULES
Cimetière de Saint-Georges
L'Arve

POI
Cathedral
Information
Airport
Railway Stn
Bus Station
Hospital
Police Stn

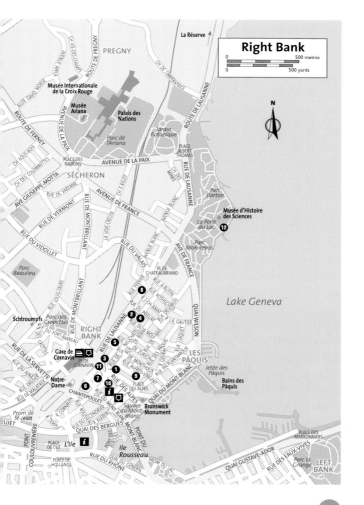

La Réserve

PREGNY

**Right Bank**

0             500 metres
0             500 yards

N

Musée Internationale
de la Croix Rouge

Musée
Ariana

Palais des
Nations

Jardin
Botanique

Parc de
l'Ariana

PLACE
ALBERT
THOMAS

PLACE DES
NATIONS

SÉCHERON

AVENUE DE LA PAIX

Parc
Barton

Musée d'Histoire
des Sciences **12**

La Perle
du Lac

Parc
Mon Repos

PL DE
CHATEAUBRIAND

**8**

Parc
Beaulieu

Schtroumpfs

Parc des
Cropettes

RIGHT
BANK

**2**
**4**

**5**

Lake Geneva

Gare de
Cornavin

**3**

**11**

**1**

**7**
**6**

**10**
**i**

**9**

LES
PÂQUIS

Jetée des
Pâquis

Bains des
Pâquis

Notre-
Dame

Square
du Mont-
Blanc

Brunswick
Monument

Prom de
St-Jean

PLACE
DE L'ÎLE **i**

L'Île

Île
Rousseau

PLACE DE
HOLLANDE

PLACE
DES
MARRONNIERS

Parc la
Grange

LEFT
BANK

where it's possible to trace the life cycle of a tree and touch different kinds of bark. As well as plant life, the gardens are home to parrots, pink flamingoes, wild goats and deer. ⓐ 1 chemin de l'Impératrice ⓣ 022 418 51 00 ⓦ www.ville-ge.ch ⓛ 08.00–19.30 Apr–Sept; 09.30–17.00 Oct–Mar ⓝ Bus: 1, 11, 28 to Jardin Botanique

### Palais des Nations (Palace of Nations)

The immense Palace of Nations is the European headquarters of the United Nations. Colourful flags line the avenue leading up to the huge building. It's worth taking a behind-the-scenes tour to glimpse some of the cavernous halls where the political action takes place. The gardens showcase the symbolic Armillary Sphere and the enormous *Broken Chair* sculpture, a protest against landmines. ⓐ 14 avenue de la Paix ⓣ 022 917 48 96 ⓦ www.unog.ch ⓛ 10.00–12.00, 14.00–16.00 Apr–Oct; 10.00–17.00 Nov–Mar ⓝ Tram: 13 to Nations

⬤ *A monument to cooperation: the Palais des Nations*

### Parc Barton

This English-style landscaped garden is dominated by the pink Villa Barton, which Sir Robert Peel acquired in the 19th century. He planted the forest of giant sequoia trees that still stands tall today. ⓐ 118 rue de Lausanne ⓝ Bus: 1 to Sécheron

### Parc Mon Repos

Centred around a stately 19th-century villa (Casanova is reputed to have stayed in an earlier house on the site), this attractive lakefront park is a pleasant place to walk through. Enjoy the lush Mediterranean gardens, admire snow-capped Mont Blanc and rest in the shade of ancient trees. ⓐ Rue de Lausanne ⓝ Bus: 1 to Sécheron

### La Perle du Lac

With its pretty perennials, mature trees and dancing fountains, this lakefront park is one of Geneva's most scenic spots in which

to relax and soak up the views. A web of paths takes in statues and clipped box hedges. In summer, the lawn is a sea of brightly coloured dahlias. The park is particularly beautiful in late afternoon when a diffused light turns the Alps various shades of pink.
ⓐ 128 rue de Lausanne ⓝ Bus: 1 to Sécheron

### Schtroumpfs (Smurfs)

While you're unlikely to see any little blue creatures here, this Gaudíesque building named after the Smurfs does indeed look as though it has stepped straight out of a comic strip. Irregular contours, wacky mosaic designs, wave-shaped balconies and larger-than-life mushrooms define this fantastical edifice in Les Grottes. The unconventional icon is one of Geneva's true hidden gems. ⓐ 23–29 rue Louis-Favre ⓝ Bus: 8 to Grottes

## CULTURE

### Musée Ariana (Ariana Museum)

Adorned with bas-reliefs and overlooking a beautiful fountain, this museum's pastel pink façade is wonderfully over the top – visit after dark to see it illuminated. The domed neoclassical building shelters an exquisite collection of ceramics and glasswork spanning seven centuries. ⓐ 10 avenue de la Paix ⓣ 022 418 54 50 ⓔ ariana@ville-ge.ch ⓛ 10.00–17.00 Wed–Mon ⓝ Bus: 8 to Appia. Admission charge

### Musée d'Histoire des Sciences (History of Science Museum)

It doesn't cost anything to unravel the wonders of science at this neoclassical mansion set in Perle du Lac park, where you can test out a range of inventions from telescopes and sundials to parabolic mirrors and microscopes. ⓐ Villa Bartholini, 128 rue de Lausanne ☎ 022 418 50 60 🕐 10.00–17.00 Wed–Mon 🚌 Bus: 1 to Sécheron

## Musée Internationale de la Croix Rouge (International Red Cross Museum)

Located opposite the Palace of Nations, this fascinating museum traces the progress of the Red Cross since its foundation in 1863. Multimedia displays take an in-depth look at the world's largest humanitarian network, with themes moving from the 'Written Word', dealing with respect for life, to 'Acts of Mercy', focusing on Florence Nightingale's benevolent deeds. Perhaps most poignant

🔺 The beautiful Villa Bartholoni, home to the Musée d'Histoire des Sciences

## SCINTILLATING SPA

If you fancy a little pampering, head for La Réserve spa.
Ranked one of the top retreats in the world, this temple of
self-indulgence overlooking Lake Geneva is the playground
of celebrities. Signature treatments include balneotherapy,
ayurvedic massage and the three-hour 'Swiss bliss' package.
It's exclusive and expensive, but the feel-good factor is worthy
of the 5 stars. ⓐ 301 route de Lausanne ⓣ 022 959 59 99
ⓦ www.lareserve.ch ⓛ 08.30–20.00 ⓛ Train: Les Tuileries

of all is the 'Wall of Time', charting epidemics, tragedies and armed
conflicts. ⓐ 17 avenue de la Paix ⓣ 022 748 95 25 ⓦ www.micr.ch
ⓛ 10.00–17.00 Wed–Mon ⓝ Tram: 13 to Nations. Admission charge

## RETAIL THERAPY

**Manor** An ideal one-stop shop close to the station, this six-level
department store is the biggest in Geneva and stocks women's
fashion, fragrances, sportswear, home design, jewellery and
lingerie. The top floor affords panoramic views from the terrace.
ⓐ 6 rue de Cornavin ⓣ 022 909 46 99 ⓦ www.manor.ch
ⓛ 09.00–19.00 Mon–Wed, 09.00–21.00 Thur, 09.00–19.30 Fri,
08.30–18.00 Sat ⓝ Tram: 13 to Cornavin

**Metro Shopping Cornavin** This mall near the station is home to
a clutch of high-street stores including Yves Rocher, Swarovski,
Lacoste and Merkur for Swiss chocolate. There's also a tea room,

bakery, sushi bar and newsagent. ⓐ 10 place de Cornavin
ⓣ 022 900 22 10 ⓦ www.metroshopping.ch ⓛ 09.00–19.00
Mon–Fri, 09.00–17.00 Sat ⓝ Tram: 13 to Cornavin

**Swatch Shop** Visit this brightly coloured store for the latest
Swatch watches in all shapes and sizes. ⓐ 19 rue du Mont-Blanc
ⓣ 022 900 22 10 ⓛ 09.00–19.00 Mon–Fri, 09.00–18.00 Sat
ⓝ Bus: 8 to Mont-Blanc

## TAKING A BREAK

**Boky £ ❶** Chefs whip up tasty and cheap Japanese, Chinese and
Malay specialities at this no-frills restaurant. ⓐ 21 rue des Alpes
ⓣ 022 738 37 94 ⓛ 11.00–02.00 ⓝ Bus: 1 to Alpes

**Maison de l'Ancre £ ❷** If you're on a tight budget, this relaxed
hospice café serves the cheapest lunch in town – from fresh
salads and sandwiches to homemade cakes and coffee.
ⓐ 34 rue de Lausanne ⓣ 022 420 58 00 ⓛ 08.00–22.15
Mon–Thur, 08.00–23.15 Fri ⓝ Tram: 13, 15 to Môle

**Il Monte Bianco £ ❸** Crammed with the finest Italian fare, from
whole hams to wines and olives, the lunchtime queue speaks
volumes for the quality. ⓐ 9 rue Chaponnière, off rue des Alpes
ⓣ 022 732 41 54 ⓛ 08.00–20.00 Mon–Fri ⓝ Tram: 13, 15 to Môle

**Só Mel £ ❹** Locals enjoy yummy Portuguese pastries at this
unpretentious tea room. ⓐ 52 rue de Lausanne ⓣ 022 732 34 58
ⓛ 06.00–19.00 Thur–Tues ⓝ Tram: 13, 15 to Môle

## AFTER DARK

### RESTAURANTS

**Café Gandhi £ 5** Decorated with red velvet, wood carvings and fairy lights, this unassuming restaurant serves tasty fish curries and dhal with fluffy naan breads. ⓐ 37 rue de Neuchâtel ⓣ 022 731 61 61 ⓦ www.gandhi.ch ⓛ 12.00–14.30, 19.00–23.00 Mon–Sat, 12.00–14.30 Sun ⓝ Bus: 1 to Monthoux

**Café de Paris £ 6** Vegetarians beware! There's only one thing on the menu at this classic French bistro – steak served with fries. It can be a bit of a squeeze to get in, but the buzz adds to the atmosphere. ⓐ 26 rue du Mont-Blanc ⓣ 022 732 84 50 ⓦ www.cafe-de-paris.ch ⓛ 11.00–23.00 ⓝ Bus: 8 to Mont-Blanc

**Restaurant Mañana £ 7** Feisty fajitas, vegetarian enchiladas and free-flowing tequila are on the menu at this Mexican-inspired restaurant above the Cactus Club. ⓐ 3 rue Chaponnière, off rue des Alpes ⓣ 022 732 21 31 ⓦ www.manana.ch ⓛ 12.00–14.00, 18.00–23.30 Mon–Sat, 18.00–23.30 Sun ⓝ Bus: 8 to Mont-Blanc

**Ze do Pipo £ 8** Tuck into *bacalhau assado* (baked cod) at this inviting little restaurant dishing up authentic Portuguese specialities. ⓐ 57 rue de Lausanne ⓣ 022 738 88 21 ⓛ 08.00–23.30 Mon–Sat ⓝ Tram: 13, 15 to Môle

**Bistrot du Boeuf Rouge ££ 9** In the heart of the trendy Pâquis district, this bistro is a blast from the past. The menu specialises in Lyonnaise fare such as *andouillette beaujolaise* (tripe sausage)

and *boudin noir* (blood sausage). ⓐ 17 rue Alfred-Vincent
ⓣ 022 732 75 37 ⓦ www.boeufrouge.ch ⓛ 12.00–14.00,
19.00–22.00 Mon–Fri ⓝ Bus: 1 to Monthoux

**La Matze ££ ⓾** This rustic restaurant evokes a snug alpine chalet.
Savour hearty fare like cheese fondue or beef charbonnade.
ⓐ 7 rue Chapponière, off rue des Alpes ⓣ 022 732 79 61
ⓦ www.la-matze.ch ⓛ 12.00–14.00, 19.00–23.00 Mon–Fri,
19.00–23.00 Sat ⓝ Bus: 8 to Mont-Blanc

**El Mektoub ££ ⓫** You'd be forgiven for thinking you were
in Marrakech at this Aladdin's cave of a restaurant. Sample
North African favourites like couscous and tender lamb
with artichokes. ⓐ 5 rue Chapponière, off rue des Alpes
ⓣ 022 738 70 31 ⓛ 12.00–00.00 Mon–Fri, 18.00–00.00 Sat
ⓝ Bus: 8 to Mont-Blanc

**La Perle du Lac £££ ⓬** The views from this stylish restaurant
are as delightful as the gourmet menu. ⓐ Parc Mon Repos
ⓣ 022 909 10 20 ⓦ www.laperledulac.ch ⓛ 11.00–01.00
ⓝ Bus: 1 to Sécheron

## BARS & CLUBS

**Cactus Club** The cocktails at this underground bar take some
beating. Bursting with young partygoers at the weekends, this
is the place to dance the night away to soulful sounds. ⓐ 3 rue
Chapponière, off rue des Alpes ⓣ 022 732 21 31 ⓦ www.manana.ch
ⓛ 18.00–01.00 Sun–Thur, 18.00–02.00 Fri & Sat ⓝ Bus: 8 to
Mont-Blanc

**Lord Jim** This cheery British pub has some decent beers on tap and is a cosy spot to catch sports on the big screen.  32 rue de Lausanne  022 732 52 92  www.lordjimpub.ch  17.00–02.00 Mon–Fri, 18.00–02.00 Sat & Sun  Tram: 13 to Môle

**Mr Pickwick Pub** This cosy English pub claims to be Switzerland's oldest. Expect the works – from 13 beers on tap to big-screen sports, live bands, karaoke and quiz nights.  80 rue de Lausanne  022 731 67 97  www.mrpickwick.ch  10.00–02.00  Tram: 13 to Butini

**New York Bar** Doubling as a restaurant, this elegant bar exudes old-world charm. You can spend a leisurely evening here sipping a bourbon or malt whisky.  24 rue du Cendrier  022 731 76 98  07.00–02.00 Mon–Sat  Bus: 29 to Chantepoulet

**Platinum Glam Club** If you're painting the Right Bank red, you'll probably wind up at this ultra-hip club where, after persuading the doormen to let you in, you'll enjoy Geneva's wildest parties.  18 quai du Seujet  022 738 90 91  www.platinum-club.ch  23.00–05.00  Tram: 16 to Isaac-Mercier

**Willi's** This upbeat lounge bar is the place to see and be seen on the fashionable rue du Mont-Blanc. The terrace is perfect for people watching.  11 rue du Mont-Blanc  022 732 77 09  willis@arthurs.ch  07.00–02.00 Mon–Fri, 08.00–02.00 Sat, 09.00–02.00 Sun  Bus: 8 to Mont-Blanc

# Carouge

Although just a 15-minute tram ride south of the centre, Carouge feels a world apart from Geneva. It was barely a speck on the map until 1754 when it became part of the Kingdom of Sardinia and King Victor Amédée III transformed the tiny hamlet into a flourishing town. The Piedmont landmarks that sprang up in the 18th century give the town its distinctly Italian atmosphere.

The beauty of Carouge lies in its understated charm and laid-back feel. While its sights might not quite rival those of other districts in Geneva, its sunny squares, pavement cafés and green-shuttered houses festooned with flower baskets ensure that it captivates nevertheless. You can easily spend a day here boutique shopping, strolling the banks of the River Arve and soaking up the local flavour in bohemian cafés. This little taste of Sardinia is still off the beaten tourist track, so discover it soon.

## SIGHTS & ATTRACTIONS

### Église Ste-Croix (St Cross Church)

This baroque cruciform church has a striking façade with slender columns, a central tower and Piedmontese elements – glance up to see the cockerel perching on the cross. An oasis of calm, the interior features grey-and-white frescoes, two rose windows and an organ dating from the romantic period. But the church's greatest claim to fame is that it houses Switzerland's largest carillon, comprising 36 bells, which you're likely to hear before you see. ⓐ Place du Marché ⓣ 022 342 26 84 ⓦ www.saintecroix.ch ⓛ 09.00–18.30 ⓝ Tram: 12, 13 to Marché

THE CITY

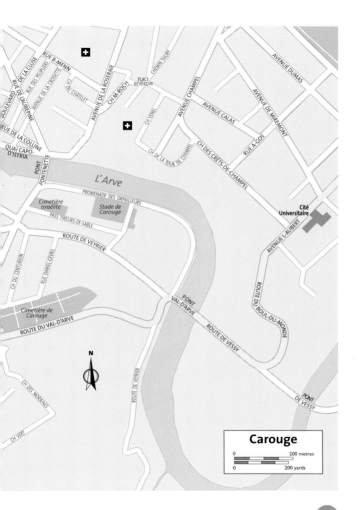

L'Arve

Cimetière Israélite

Stade de Carouge

Cimetière de Carouge

Cité Universitaire

**Carouge**

0         200 metres

0         200 yards

## Mairie (Town Hall)

Squatting in the shadow of the church, the town hall is the brainchild of Italian architect Giuseppe Piacenza. The sandy-coloured structure was built in 1777 as a presbytery and today it proudly flies the Carouge flag (a white lion beside a tree set against a red background). It is not open for visiting. ⓐ 14 place du Marché ⓦ www.carouge.ch ⓝ Tram: 12, 13 to Marché

🔺 *The elegant Église Ste-Croix*

**Maisons Artisanales (Craftsmen's Houses)**
Once home to the town's craftsmen, these Mediterranean-inspired houses are some of the best-preserved examples of 18th-century architecture in Carouge. Take a peek at their twisting staircases, arcades and leafy inner courtyards. ⓐ 8–30 rue Ancienne ⓛ 14.00–18.00 Tues–Sun ⓝ Tram: 12, 13 to Marché

**Place du Marché (Market Square)**
The epicentre of Carouge life, this picture-perfect square is fringed with plane trees and overshadowed by the church. Be sure to look at the Blavignac fountain, a tribute to the River Arve shaped from rock and bronze. The twice-weekly market (see page 97) injects life into the square and a string of pavement cafés and restaurants reel in locals and visitors. It's a great spot to enjoy lunch or coffee and indulge in some prime people watching. ⓝ Tram: 12, 13 to Marché

**Pont-Neuf**
With its trio of limestone arches, this bridge bears an uncanny resemblance to its namesake in Paris. Although the river has washed it away several times in the past, the current bridge, dating back to 1817, is built of sterner stuff. From here you can admire the silver-grey waters of the meandering River Arve, a tributary of the Rhône that's fed by alpine glaciers. It's possible to stroll along the river's tree-lined banks and, if you're lucky, spot herons and beavers. ⓝ Tram: 12, 13 to Armes

**Temple**
Quite aptly named temple, this neoclassical church boasts

peristyle columns and a Grecian-style pediment. Built in the early 19th century, this gem includes Byzantine-style wood carvings and elaborately frescoed vaults. It is open for guided tours and Sunday morning services only. ⓐ Place du Temple ⓛ Guided tours: 08.00–13.00 Wed & Sat ⓝ Tram: 12, 13 to Marché

⬤ *Take a tour of the neoclassical Temple*

## CULTURE

### Musée de Carouge (Carouge Museum)

The imposing 18th-century Montanrouge House shelters this intriguing museum, which provides an insight into Carouge life past and present. Alongside temporary exhibitions, the permanent collection features a clutch of ceramics, paintings, art deco crafts and contemporary works by Carouge artists. Be sure to take a look at the Sardinian garden while you're there. ⓐ 2 place de Sardaigne ⓣ 022 342 33 83 ⓦ www.carouge.ch ⓛ 14.00–18.00 Tues–Sun ⓝ Tram: 12, 13 to Marché

### Théâtre de Carouge (Carouge Theatre)

Experimental productions, cutting-edge plays and perennial favourites take to the stage of Carouge's intimate theatre, which was founded in 1958. ⓐ 57 rue Ancienne ⓣ 022 343 43 43 ⓦ www.theatredecarouge-geneve.ch ⓛ 19.00 Tues, Thur & Sat, 20.00 Wed & Fri, 17.00 Sun ⓝ Tram: 13 to Carouge

## RETAIL THERAPY

**Asaya** This dinky boutique is crammed with Indonesian crafts, from multicoloured elephants to intricate woodcarvings. ⓐ 16 rue Ancienne ⓣ 022 301 93 60 ⓛ 07.00–14.30 Mon–Fri, 08.45–14.30 Sat ⓝ Tram: 13 to Carouge

**Auteur du Bain** There is a whiff of nostalgia in this quirky shop, where tin tubs brim with dreamy bath products. Natural ingredients are used to create heart-shaped soaps on sticks and edible-looking bath sweets, cakes, chocolates, puddings and confetti. Lotions and potions scented with Moroccan rose, Egyptian jasmine and amber will make you want to run a bath straight away. ⓐ 12 rue Saint-Joseph ① 022 300 52 73 ① 10.00–12.30, 14.00–19.00 Tues–Fri, 10.00–19.00 Sat ② Tram: 12, 13 to Marché

**Betjeman & Barton** The red walls are lined with every type of tea, teapot and cup imaginable at this cha-crazy store. A unique brew to look out for is *La Dame du Lac*, a blend of Mirabelle plum,

## CRAFTY CAROUGE

Carouge's creative roots stretch back to the 18th century, when the town was home to a plethora of carpenters, cobblers, blacksmiths, dressmakers, tanneries and watchmakers. The arty spirit is still alive and kicking today; the narrow streets a maze of musty antique shops, Lilliputian galleries and boutiques that are full of curiosities, original handicrafts and one-off local designs.

As you amble through the town, you'll come across the workshops and boutiques of potters, glassblowers, ceramicists, jewellers, hatters, fashion designers, *chocolatiers* and confectioners. The beauty of shopping here is that you can often meet the makers themselves, and discover the raw materials and processes that go into their work. If you want high-street names and designer labels, stick to Geneva centre; but if you're seeking arty gifts, it has got to be crafty Carouge.

strawberry, apple and caramel. You'll also find fresh ginger juice and lavender confiture here. ⓐ 35 rue Saint-Joseph ⓣ 022 301 20 30 ⓦ www.barton.ch ⓛ 09.45–17.30 Mon–Fri, 09.45–13.00, 14.00–17.00 Sat ⓝ Tram: 12, 13 to Marché

**Bignens Vins** This intoxicating store offers a staggering choice of regional and world wines. ⓐ 2 rue du Marché ⓣ 022 301 75 40 ⓦ www.bignens.ch ⓛ 08.30–12.30, 14.00–18.45 Mon–Sat ⓝ Tram: 12, 13 to Marché

**Farmers' Market** Taking over the main square twice a week, this market serves up voluptuous fruits, bunches of fresh lavender, farm-fresh Reblochon, handmade breads, truffles, homemade preserves and honey. Even if you don't plan to buy, come to soak up the buzzing atmosphere and taste local wines. ⓐ Place du Marché ⓛ 08.00–13.00 Wed & Sat ⓝ Tram: 12, 13 to Marché

**Karavan Seray** From mosaic vases to leatherwork and intricate woodcarvings, this shop stocks quality crafts from Tunisia, Morocco and Algeria. ⓐ 22 rue Saint-Joseph ⓣ 022 343 96 11 ⓛ 10.00–18.30 Mon–Fri, 09.30–17.00 Sat ⓝ Tram: 13 to Carouge

**Paloma de la Paz** Pick up arty gifts like ceramics, tapestries and candles in this boutique. ⓐ 42 rue Ancienne ⓣ 022 342 61 98 ⓛ 07.00–14.30 Mon–Fri, 08.45–14.30 Sat ⓝ Tram: 13 to Carouge

**Philippe Pascoët** Master *chocolatier* Philippe Pascoët pours his passion and know-how into creating Carouge's finest chocolates. The cocoa-rich pralines and truffles are infused with herbs like

fresh mint, basil, star anis, rosemary, sage and even tobacco.
 22 rue Saint-Joseph  022 301 20 58  www.philippe-pascoet.ch
 10.00–18.30 Mon–Fri, 09.30–17.00 Sat  Tram: 12, 13 to Marché

**Verrerie Berlin Artisanale** It may look like marble or precious
stones, but everything in this pocket-sized boutique is handcrafted
from glass.  4 rue Saint-Joseph  022 343 10 43  15.00–18.30
Tues–Fri, 09.00–12.00 Sat  Tram: 12, 13 to Marché

**Zabo** Hat lovers should visit this kooky boutique and workshop;
it has colourful creations from the woolly to the wacky that
will make you stand out from the crowd.  31 rue Saint-Joseph
 022 301 75 76  www.zabo.ch  14.00–18.30 Tues–Fri,
10.00–12.30, 14.00–17.00 Sat  Tram: 12, 13 to Marché

## TAKING A BREAK

**Café de l'Aigle £ ❶** Shabby chic sums up this convivial
café, where the walls are graced with arty shots of India.
It's a pleasant spot for a light lunch or drinks with the locals
at the bar.  42 rue Ancienne  022 342 61 98  07.00–14.30
Mon–Fri, 08.45–14.30 Sat  Tram: 13 to Carouge

**Calm £ ❷** It's easy to see the appeal of this effortlessly cool
café: jazzy lounge music, delicious home-grown food and
a relaxed vibe that will indeed leave you feeling very calm.
Snacks include goat's-cheese quiche, yoghurt cake, warming
soups and fresh-pressed juices. With wood beams, flickering
candles and squishy leather chairs, the lounge is a great place

to hibernate. **ⓐ** 36 rue Ancienne **ⓣ** 022 301 22 20 **ⓛ** 07.00–14.30 Mon–Fri, 08.00–14.30 Sat **ⓝ** Tram: 13 to Carouge

**Gelato Mania £ ❸** When the weather is warm, the handmade ice cream and sorbets at this hole-in-the-wall gelateria are refreshing. **ⓐ** 43 rue Saint-Joseph **ⓔ** gelatomania@bluewin.ch **ⓛ** 12.00–23.00 Tues–Thur, 11.00–00.00 Fri–Sun, May–Aug; 12.00–18.00 Tues–Sun, Sept & Oct **ⓝ** Tram: 12, 13 to Marché

**Martel £ ❹** Avid chocolate lovers should make for this *confiserie* which serves mouth-watering pralines, éclairs, glistening strawberry tarts and bite-sized petits fours. Sample them in the elegant tearoom **ⓐ** 8 rue du Marché **ⓣ** 022 342 00 45 **ⓛ** 07.30–19.00 Tues–Fri, 07.30–18.00 Sat & Sun **ⓝ** Tram: 12, 13 to Marché

**Wolfisberg £ ❺** The smell of freshly baked bread fills the air at this spacious pâtisserie and tearoom in the centre of town. The design is contemporary with bright colours, and the baguettes and pastries are superb. **ⓐ** 5 place du Temple **ⓣ** 022 342 32 19 **ⓛ** 06.30–19.00 Thur–Tues **ⓝ** Tram: 12, 13 to Marché

## AFTER DARK

### RESTAURANTS
**Au Boccalino £ ❻** Red-checked tablecloths, tiled floors and beamed ceilings give this cave-like restaurant the feel of a rustic Italian trattoria. The well-prepared antipasti, wood-fired pizza and fresh salads served with Chianti would make mamma proud.

**a** 4 place du Rondeau **t** 022 343 73 87 **e** leboccalino@bluewin.ch
**l** 11.00–14.00, 18.30–23.00 **n** Tram: 13 to Carouge

**La Bourse £ ❼** At the heart of Carouge, this classic brasserie
is all brick, warm wood and soft lighting. Pull up
a chair in the frescoed cellar and choose between favourites
such as *marmite du pêcheur* (fish casserole), champagne
fondue and Bourgogne snails. The prix-fixe menu is chalked
up on a blackboard. **a** 7 place du Marché **t** 022 342 04 66
**l** 12.00–14.00, 19.00–23.00 Mon–Sat **n** Tram: 12, 13 to Marché

**Carlito £ ❽** The menu is predominantly Swiss at this snug
wood-panelled bistro next to the church. The number of *rösti*
potato specialities is staggering and the four-cheese fondue
comes recommended. **a** 7 rue du Marché **t** 022 300 26 56
**l** 11.00–14.00, 18.00–22.00 **n** Tram: 12, 13 to Marché

**La Cave £ ❾** The walls are lined with gleaming wine bottles
at this cosy enclave, where fondue burners glow on the tables.
With specialities like tomato fondue and meringues with
Gruyère cream there's no point counting the calories here.
**a** 42 rue Saint-Joseph **t** 022 300 50 06 **l** 18.00–23.00 Mon–Sat
**n** Tram: 12, 13 to Marché

**Épiaprès £ ❿** Mediterranean touches and fusion cuisine are
the big draw here. After dark, the inviting café transforms into
a vibrant restaurant serving tasty Spanish tapas and waistline-
expanding Swiss treats such as chocolate fondue with fresh
fruit. **a** 37 rue Saint-Joseph **t** 022 342 03 32 **w** www.epiapres.ch

🕐 06.00–00.00 Mon–Fri, 10.00–00.00 Sat Ⓝ Tram: 12, 13
to Marché

**Au Lion d'Or de Carouge £ ⓫** Housed in a 300-year-old building,
this unpretentious little restaurant draws locals who come for
the flavoursome food and great-value *plat du jour*. Take a seat in
the vaulted cellar or in the pretty courtyard to savour a fusion of
French and Italian flavours with dishes such as risotto and duck
foie gras with cider apples. ⓐ 53 rue Ancienne ⓣ 022 342 18 13
Ⓦ www.liondor-carouge.ch 🕐 12.00–13.30, 19.00–22.30 Mon–Fri
Ⓝ Tram: 13 to Carouge

**La Table ££ ⓬** Serious foodies are in for a treat at this stylish,
light-filled restaurant close to the main square. It may look
unassuming from outside, but it's the kitchen that counts.
Dishes like curried salmon and tender lamb with ratatouille
keep people coming back for more. ⓐ 31 rue Jacques-Dalphin
ⓣ 022 301 13 22 🕐 16.00–02.00 Mon–Sat Ⓝ Tram: 12, 13
to Marché

## BARS & CLUBS

**Le Chat Noir** If you want to get your claws into Carouge's after-
dark scene, head for the black cat. Staging some of Geneva's
hottest live music, the cellar of this hip venue resounds with
everything from jazz to rock concerts, chanson and operetta.
DJs on the decks keep the tiny dance floor crammed until the
early hours of the morning. ⓐ 13 rue Vautier ⓣ 022 343 49 98
Ⓦ www.chatnoir.ch 🕐 18.00–04.00 Mon–Thur, 18.00–05.00
Fri & Sat Ⓝ Tram: 12, 13 to Marché

**L'Imprévu** Black leather chairs, wood floors and original art make this a laid-back spot in which to enjoy a cappuccino by day or cocktail by night – try a Mojito or Cuba Libre. ⓐ 37–39 rue Vautier ⓣ 022 343 77 00 ⓛ 08.00–01.00 Mon–Fri, 08.00–02.00 Sat ⓝ Tram: 12, 13 to Marché

**Lion Rouge Pub** This good old-fashioned pub is as far removed from 'posh' Geneva as they come. The cosy den is kitted out with a red telephone box and offers an arm-long list of beers including Amstel, Kilkenny and Erdinger. ⓐ 2 rue de Veyrier ⓣ 022 343 55 07 ⓛ 16.00–02.00 Mon–Sat ⓝ Tram: 12, 13 to Marché

**Qu'importe** Inspired by Alfred de Musset's phrase, '*Qu'importe le flacon...*', this funky lounge bar is a popular spot. Sink into the chocolate-hued leather sofas to unwind with a glass of wine and tapas by the fire. The terrace hums with life in summer. ⓐ 1 rue Ancienne ⓣ 022 342 15 25 ⓔ contact@quimporte.ch ⓛ 08.00–01.00 Tues–Thur, 08.00–02.00 Fri & Sat ⓝ Tram: 12, 13 to Ancienne

---

▶ *Boats and battlements at Annecy*

OUT OF TOWN
trips

# Lausanne

Capital of the canton of Vaud, Lausanne is an effervescent
university city that boasts pristine Belle Époque architecture,
a hilltop medieval Old Town and a glut of vibrant bars.

## GETTING THERE

The A1 motorway links Geneva to Lausanne and the journey
takes 45 minutes by car. The city is also easy to reach by public
transport, with SBB trains departing frequently from Geneva's
main station with a journey time of approximately 45 minutes.
The easiest way to travel from Geneva by bus is to take bus
numbers 10 or 18 from Aéroport Genève-Cointrin (see page 50)
which leave every 30 minutes from 08.00–20.00. In summer, a
pleasant way to arrive is by ferry – contact **CGN** (ⓦ www.cgn.ch)
for further details. The public transport details given in this
chapter refer to connections in Lausanne, not connections
from Geneva to the city.

## SIGHTS & ATTRACTIONS

### Cathédrale de Notre-Dame (Notre-Dame Cathedral)
Lausanne's Gothic cathedral looms large above the Old Town.
Inside, light pierces the 13th-century rose window and imbues
the interior with a sense of calm. For sweeping views over the
city's rooftops, head for the terrace. ⓐ Place de la Cathédrale
ⓣ 021 316 71 61 ⓛ 07.00–19.00 Mon–Fri, 08.00–19.00 Sat & Sun
ⓝ Bus: 16 to Pierre-Viret

### Château Saint-Maire (Saint-Maire Castle)

The spires of this 14th-century red-brick castle are like something out of a classic fairy tale. One-time home of bishops and Bernese bailiffs, it is now the seat of the cantonal government. The terrace affords far-reaching views over the city. ⓐ Place du Château ⓣ 022 342 26 84 ⓛ 10.00–19.00 Mon–Fri Ⓝ Bus: 16 to Pierre-Viret

### Hôtel de Ville (Town Hall)

The epicentre of Lausanne's Old Town, this arcaded Renaissance building overlooks the Fountain of Justice – get there on the hour to see historical figurines parade from the clock on the wall behind. It is not open for visiting. ⓐ Place de la Palud ⓣ 022 342 26 84 Ⓝ Bus: 16 to Pierre-Viret

⬥ Parade on the promenade at Ouchy

**Geneva region**

| 0 | 10 km |
| 0 | 5 miles |

La Chaux-du-Dombief
Pont-de-Poitte
Clairvaux-les-Lacs
Orgelet
JURA
Varennes-St-Sauveur
Cuiseaux
Chambéria
Charchilla
Revermont
Lac de Vouglans
Bienne
A39
St-Amour
St-Julien
Arinthod
St-Claude
Coligny
Septmoncel
Ain
St-Étienne-du-Bois
Dortan
Viry
Les Bouchoux
Revermont
Surran
Ain
Thoirette
Crêt de la Neige 1718 ▲
Treffort-Cuisiat
Viriat
Izernore
Oyonnax
Semine
Bourg-en-Bresse
A404
Mont Burdet 1043 ▲
FRANCE
Valserine
Péron
Cevzériat
St-Martin-du-Frêne
Nantua
Le Grand Crêt d'Eau 1621 ▲
A40
Lent
Châtillon-en-Michaille
Collonges
St-Martin-du-Mont
AIN
Bellegarde-sur-Valserine
A40
Oignin
Ponein
Crêt des Éculaz 1014
Crêt du Nu 1351
Rhône
A42
Jujurieux
Brénod
Frangy
Châtillon-la-Palud
Lyon
Ambronay
Albarine
Ruffieu
Bassy
Germany
France
Switzerland
St-Rambert-en-Bugey
Seran
Seyssel
Thusy
Geneva region
Italy
Cluse des Hôpitaux
Champagne-en-Valromey
Grand Colombier 1531 ▲
Artemare
Fur
Rumilly
Villebois
Ruffieux

### Jardin Botanique (Botanical Gardens)

Steep paths weave through these hilltop botanical gardens, which are home to 6,000 species, including medicinal, alpine and tropical plants. From the top there are 360° views over Lausanne and the lake. ⓐ Avenue de Beauregard ⓣ 021 316 99 88 ⓦ www.botanique.vd.ch ⓛ 10.00–17.30 Mar–Oct ⓝ Bus: 1 to Beauregard

### Ouchy

The port of Ouchy is a far cry from the city's bustle: the waterfront promenade is where the locals come to relax, stroll and drink in views of the Alps. Fringed with flower-strewn gardens, the quays are home to grand hotels, smart restaurants, the Olympic Park and a castle. Boats bobbing in the marina, candyfloss sellers, carousels and street entertainers give it a seaside feel. ⓐ Quai d'Ouchy ⓝ Bus: 2 to Navigation

## CULTURE

### Fondation de l'Hermitage

Situated in the Bois de Sauvabelin park, this pink 19th-century residence houses an exceptional permanent collection featuring works by Degas, Sisley and Magritte. The gallery frequently hosts temporary exhibitions too. ⓐ 2 route du Signal ⓣ 021 320 50 01 ⓦ www.fondation-hermitage.ch ⓛ 11.00–18.00 Tues–Sun ⓝ Bus: 3 to Motte. Admission charge

### Musée Historique (History Museum)

This intriguing museum opposite the cathedral traces Lausanne's history from the Ice Age to the 20th century. Low-beamed rooms and narrow passageways are the backdrop for chronological displays that include Neolithic skeletons, religious iconography, silverware and antique musical instruments. ⓐ 4 place de la Cathédrale ⓣ 021 315 41 01 ⓦ www.lausanne.ch/mhl ⓛ 11.00–18.00 Tues–Thur, 11.00–17.00 Fri–Sun ⓝ Bus: 16 to Pierre-Viret. Admission charge

### Musée Olympique (Olympic Museum)
Shaped from marble and soaring above the Olympic Park on Ouchy embankment, this monumental building is a tribute to Lausanne's Olympic heritage – the city has been home to the International Olympic Committee (IOC) since 1915. Themed displays cover all aspects of the Games. ⓐ Quai d'Ouchy ⓣ 021 621 65 11 ⓦ www.olympic.org ⓛ 09.00–18.00 Apr–Oct; 09.00–18.00 Tues–Sun, Nov–Mar ⓝ Bus: 8 to Musée Olympique. Admission charge

### Opéra de Lausanne (Lausanne Opera)
The acclaimed Lausanne Opera presents an eclectic repertoire of opera, dance, classical concerts and recitals. The season runs from September to May. ⓐ 12 avenue du Théâtre ⓣ 021 310 16 00 ⓦ www.opera-lausanne.ch ⓛ 09.00–18.30 ⓝ Bus: 9, 12 to Georgette

### Palais de Rumine (Rumine Palace)
The sheer scale of this neo-Renaissance building towering above place de la Riponne is impressive. The ornate façade shelters a clutch of fascinating museums, including the Fine Arts Museum, the Archaeology & History Museum, and the

Zoological Museum. Highlights include the reconstruction of a Neolithic cave and masterpieces by Swiss artist Charles Gleyre. ⓐ Place de la Riponne ⓣ 021 692 44 70 ⓒ 11.00–18.00 Tues–Thur, 11.00–17.00 Fri–Sun ⓝ Bus: 5, 6, 8 to Riponne. Admission charge

⬥ *The magnificent Palais de Rumine*

## RETAIL THERAPY

**Art Suisse** Contemporary creations by Swiss artists are the big draw here. 🄰 8 rue Enning 🄣 021 320 81 80 🄻 12.30–18.15 Tues–Fri, 09.30–17.00 Sat 🄽 Bus: 17 to Benjamin-Constant

**Durig** Cocoa-mad Dan Durig creates divine sweets including Venezuelan milk truffles and organic chocolate plums. 🄰 15 avenue d'Ouchy 🄣 021 601 24 35 🄦 www.durig.ch 🄻 08.30–18.30 Tues–Fri, 08.30–17.00 Sat 🄽 Bus: 2 to Closelet

**La Ferme Vaudoise** Near the town hall, this store is well stocked with Vaud specialities, from Mont d'Or cheese to handmade sausages. 🄰 5 place de la Palud 🄣 021 351 35 55 🄻 09.00–13.00, 14.00–18.30 Mon–Fri, 07.30–17.00 Sat 🄽 Bus: 16 to Pierre-Viret

**L'Herboriste** This old-world shop is crammed with herbal teas, remedies, natural cosmetics, fragrances and essential oils. 🄰 12 avenue du Léman 🄣 021 311 81 70 🄦 www.lherboriste.ch 🄻 14.00–19.00 Mon, 14.30–19.00 Tues–Fri, 09.00–17.00 Sat 🄽 Bus: 9 to avenue du Léman

**TheTeaTee** Around 160 blends of tea and delicate china line the walls of this inviting shop. Look out for the exclusive Me Tseng vintage. 🄰 4 rue Enning 🄣 021 312 48 63 🄦 www.theteatee.ch 🄻 13.30–18.30 Mon, 09.30–18.30 Tues–Fri, 09.30–17.00 Sat 🄽 Bus: 17 to Benjamin-Constant

## TAKING A BREAK

**Délices du Chocolat £** The sweet-toothed should make for this smart tearoom for luscious apple tarts, petits fours and pastries. Pick up some cocoa-dusted truffles on your way out. ⓐ 2–4 rue Enning ⓣ 02 320 24 24 ⓛ 07.00–19.00 Mon–Fri, 07.00–18.00 Sat, 07.00–13.00 Sun ⓝ Bus: 17 to Benjamin-Constant

**L'Éléphant Blanc £** In the heart of the Old Town, this charming restaurant's menu is limited but superbly cooked, from duck foie gras to crème brulée. ⓐ 4 rue Cité-Devant ⓣ 021 312 71 77 ⓛ 11.00–00.00 Mon–Fri ⓝ Bus: 16 to Pierre-Viret

ⓞ *Specially for the sweet-toothed: Délices du Chocolat*

**Fox Café £** This spacious New York-style diner serves up tasty omelettes, curries, pasta dishes and mussels. ⓐ 10 rue Enning ⓣ 021 323 32 18 ⓛ 07.30–01.00 Mon–Thur, 07.30–02.00 Fri & Sat, 17.00–01.00 Sun ⓝ Bus: 17 to Benjamin-Constant

## AFTER DARK

### RESTAURANTS
**Café Romand £** Enjoy cheese fondue at this elegant Swiss brasserie, which has high ceilings, moody lighting and wood panelling. ⓐ 2 place Saint-François ⓣ 021 312 63 75 ⓦ www.caferomand.com ⓛ 09.00–01.00 Mon–Sat ⓝ Bus: 2, 4, 8 to St-François

**Au Couscous £** Glammed up with oriental mosaics, this hole-in-the-wall restaurant is a well-kept secret. Savour Lebanese mezze, merguez and sticky baklava. ⓐ 2 rue Enning ⓣ 021 321 38 48 ⓦ www.au-couscous.ch ⓛ 11.30–14.30, 18.30–01.00 Mon–Sat, 18.30–00.00 Sun ⓝ Bus: 17 to Benjamin-Constant

**Le Java £** This galleried restaurant fuses arabesque touches with art deco nostalgia. The menu is equally inspired. ⓐ 26 rue Marterey ⓣ 021 321 38 37 ⓦ www.lejava.ch ⓛ 08.00–00.00 Mon–Fri, 08.00–02.00 Sat & Sun ⓝ Bus: 17 to Benjamin-Constant

**À la Pomme de Pin ££** Tucked down a street near the cathedral, this brasserie serves classic specialities. ⓐ 11–13 rue Cité-Derrière ⓣ 021 323 46 56 ⓛ 08.00–00.00 Mon–Fri, 18.00–00.00 Sat ⓝ Bus: 16 to Pierre-Viret

## BARS & CLUBS

**Bleu Lezard** One of Lausanne's hippest haunts, this upbeat bar draws a lively crowd. 10 rue Enning 021 323 00 55 www.bleulezard.ch 07.00–01.00 Mon–Thur, 07.00–02.00 Fri, 08.00–02.00 Sat, 09.30–01.00 Sun Bus: 17 to Benjamin-Constant

**Les Brasseurs** Copper vats and wood floors make this micro-brewery an inviting place to enjoy a beer and some sauerkraut. 4 rue Centrale 021 351 14 24 www.les-brasseurs.ch 11.00–01.00 Mon–Thur, 11.00–02.00 Fri & Sat, 16.00–00.00 Sun Bus: 2 to Bel-Air

**Captain Cook Pub** This cheery English pub serves real ales and bar food and shows big-screen sports. 2 rue Enning 021 323 00 55 www.captain-cook.ch 08.30–01.00 Mon–Thur, 08.30–02.00 Fri, 14.00–02.00 Sat, 16.00–01.00 Sun Bus: 17 to Benjamin-Constant

**D'Club** Party till dawn to live acts and electro-house music at this funky club. 15 place Centrale 021 351 51 40 www.dclub.ch 21.00–02.00 Wed, 21.00–04.00 Thur, 21.00–05.00 Fri & Sat Bus: 2 to Bel-Air

**Le Lounge** Part of Ouchy's medieval château, this lounge-style bar affords uninterrupted views of the lake through floor-to-ceiling glass windows. 2 place du Port 021 616 74 51 www.chateaudouchy.ch 09.00–01.00 Mon–Thur, 09.00–02.00 Fri & Sat, 16.00–00.00 Sun Bus: 2 to Ouchy

## ACCOMMODATION

**Camping Vidy £** A stone's throw from Ouchy, this lakefront campsite has a supermarket, play area, laundry and restaurant. **ⓐ** 3 chemin du Camping **ⓣ** 021 622 50 00 **ⓦ** www.campinglausannevidy.ch **ⓛ** Apr–Oct **ⓝ** Bus: 2 to Bois de Vaux

**Lausanne YH £** Set in attractive grounds by the lake, this hostel features clean and bright singles, doubles and dorms. **ⓐ** 36 chemin du Bois-du-Vaux **ⓣ** 021 626 02 22 **ⓦ** www.youthhostel.ch **ⓝ** Bus: 2 to Bois de Vaux

**Hôtel Élite ££** Surrounded by gardens, this recently renovated hotel is one of Lausanne's best mid-range options. Choose the top floor for lake views. **ⓐ** 1 avenue Sainte-Luce **ⓣ** 021 320 23 61 **ⓦ** www.elite-lausanne.ch **ⓝ** Bus: 2, 4, 8 to St-François

### VINE TIME
At the heart of vine-clad Vaud, the precipitous terraces surrounding Lausanne are prime wine-growing territory. A great way to explore them is to don walking boots or hire a bicycle, pausing in the cellars en route. The 33-km (20-mile) stretch from Ouchy to Chillon passes through villages like Lutry, Riex and Chardonne and will give you intoxicating alpine views.

# Annecy

Situated on the northern tip of turquoise Lake Annecy, it's easy to see Annecy's appeal: pure alpine waters framed by jagged peaks, flower-lined canals and a medieval castle overshadowing the Old Town's warren of cobbled streets. Life here is laid-back, and simple pleasures like savouring fresh lake trout or strolling on waterfront promenades are a delight. For those seeking more adventure, Annecy's big and beautiful backyard provides a range of outdoor action including kayaking, climbing and skiing in the nearby Alps.

## GETTING THERE

The speedy A41 motorway links Geneva to Annecy in just 40 minutes. The French town is also accessible by public transport, with SNCF trains operating a frequent service to Annecy's main station. **Sibra buses** (Ⓦ www.sibra.fr) serve the town and surrounding villages. The public transport details given in this chapter refer to connections in Annecy, not connections from Geneva to the city.

## SIGHTS & ATTRACTIONS

### Basilique de la Visitation

On top of a wooded hill, this early 20th-century basilica features a striking 72 m (236 ft) steeple and offers sweeping views over Annecy. ⓐ 20 avenue de la Visitation ⓣ 04 50 45 22 76 ⓔ musees@anglo-annecy.fr ⓛ 07.00–12.00, 14.00–19.00 Ⓝ Bus: 14 to Visitation

◆ *The turquoise tranquillity of Lake Annecy*

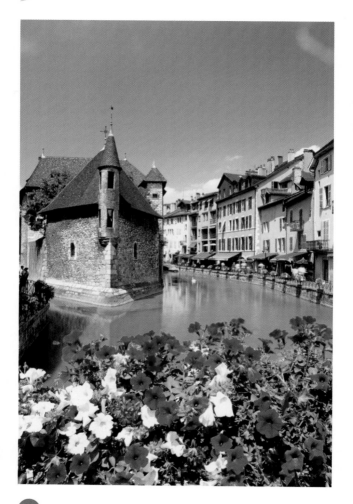

### Château d'Annecy (Annecy Castle)

Set against a backdrop of snow-capped mountains, this red-turreted castle looms large above Annecy. Sturdy towers soar above the cobbled inner courtyard, the oldest dating back to the 13th century. From this fairy-tale perch, you can enjoy superb views of the lake and town. ⓐ Place du Château ⓣ 04 50 33 87 30 ⓔ musees@anglo-annecy.fr ⓛ 10.00–12.00, 14.00–17.00 Wed–Mon, Oct–May; 10.30–18.00 June–Sept ⓝ Bus: 7, 14 to Paradis

### Jardins de l'Europe

Locals hang out by the lake's edge in these pristine gardens, which have plenty of shady nooks in which to relax and watch the world go by. Enjoy a picnic beneath the shady trees, stroll to Lovers' Bridge and glimpse the tiny Île des Cygnes (Swan Island). ⓐ Quai Napoleon III ⓝ Bus: 6, 7, 15 to Hôtel de Ville

### Palais de l'Île

Annecy's picture-perfect landmark belies its function as the town's former prison. With its wistful turrets rising high above the Thiou Canal, this medieval icon is one of France's most photographed buildings. Step inside to explore a labyrinth of cells and wander the banks to watch local artists at work. After dark, the illuminated prison is enchanting. ⓐ 3 passage de l'Île ⓣ 04 50 33 87 30 ⓔ musees@anglo-annecy.fr ⓛ 10.00–12.00, 14.00–17.00 Wed–Mon, Oct–May; 10.30–18.00 June–Sept ⓝ Bus: 6, 7, 15 to Hôtel de Ville. Admission charge

---

◐ *From town gaol to tourist delight: Palais de l'Île*

**Pont des Amours (Lovers' Bridge)**
Straddling the Vassé Canal, this arched bridge links the Jardins de l'Europe to Champs de Mars promenade. Romantic couples come here to walk hand in hand; singletons can fall in love with the views of Lake Annecy instead. ⓐ Champs de Mars ⓝ Bus: 6, 7, 15 to Hôtel de Ville

## CULTURE

**Musée Château d'Annecy (Annecy Castle Museum)**
Housed in the castle, this museum traces Annecy's intriguing history, with its displays of traditional Savoy furniture, contemporary art and alpine anthropology. ⓐ Place du Château ⓣ 04 50 33 87 30 ⓔ musees@anglo-annecy.fr ⓗ 10.00–12.00, 14.00–17.00 Wed–Mon, Oct–May; 10.30–18.00 June–Sept ⓝ Bus: 7, 14 to Paradis. Admission charge

## RECREATION

**Bateaux Dupraz** A mini-cruise is a relaxed way to tour the glistening lake and see the sights from the water. Boats with

### KING OF 12 CASTLES…
Passing through Annecy, the Road of the Dukes of Savoy links 12 historic castles, abbeys and forts. As well as tracing the region's fascinating heritage, the route takes in some spectacular alpine scenery.
ⓦ www.chateaux-france.com/route-savoie

⬥ *From pedaloes to paragliding, Annecy provides a range of diversions*

guided commentary depart regularly in summer. @ Jardins de l'Europe **①** 04 50 52 42 99 **Ⓦ** www.bateauxdupraz.com **Ⓛ** 11.00, 14.15, 15.00, 16.15, 17.15 May–Sept **Ⓝ** Bus: 6, 7, 15 to Hôtel de Ville

**Gorges du Fier** A 15-minute journey from Annecy, Lovagny boasts one of France's most dramatic river gorges. This precipitous ravine's bizarre rock formations and high footbridges are very impressive. @ Lovagny **①** 04 50 46 23 07 **Ⓦ** www.gorgesdufier.com **Ⓛ** 09.15–18.00 Mar–Oct **Ⓝ** Bus: 62 to Lovagny. Admission charge

**LocaLoisirs** This centre in nearby Annecy-le-Vieux rents kayaks, mountain bikes and scooters, as well as organising activities like paragliding, rafting and canoeing. @ 47 avenue du Petit Port **①** 04 50 23 31 15 **Ⓦ** www.annecy-loca-loisirs.com **Ⓛ** 09.00–19.00 Apr–Oct **Ⓝ** Bus: 15 to Annecy-le-Vieux/Pré Vernet

**Marquisats Swimming Pool and Beach** With its trio of outdoor pools, this lido by the lake is the ideal spot to swim and relax in summer. @ 29 rue des Marquisats **①** 04 50 33 65 40 **Ⓛ** 09.00–19.30 Mon–Fri, 09.00–19.00 Sat, 10.00–19.00 Sun, May–Sept **Ⓝ** Bus: 6, 7, 14 to Hôpital Marquisats. Admission charge

**Takamaka** Adrenaline junkies enjoy activities like canyoning, sky diving, downhill mountain biking and paragliding at this extreme sports centre. @ 23 Faubourg Sainte-Claire **①** 04 50 45 60 61 **Ⓦ** www.takamaka.fr **Ⓛ** 09.00–19.00 Apr–Oct **Ⓝ** Bus: 4, 7 to Fauré

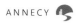

## RETAIL THERAPY

**Courier** This modern shopping mall shelters 40 high-street stores under its glass roof, including names like H&M, Fnac and Sephora. ⓐ 65 rue Carnot ⓣ 04 50 46 46 76 ⓦ www.centre-courier.com ⓛ 09.30–19.30 Mon–Sat ⓝ Bus: 2, 6, 10 to Courier

**Crèmerie du Lac Cheese** Fans of *fromage* sniff out Alain Michel's store, crammed with different cheeses. Look out for Savoy classics like flavoursome Reblochon and Roquefort ripened in a cool cellar. ⓐ 3 rue du Lac ⓣ 04 50 45 19 31 ⓦ www.cremeriedulac.com ⓛ 09.30–19.30 Mon–Sat ⓝ Bus: 6, 7, 15 to Hôtel de Ville

**Farmers' Market** Potter around Annecy's vibrant market, where stalls are piled high with local produce, from wheels of Savoy cheese to fresh fruit, plump olives, sausages and handmade bread. ⓐ Rue de la République, rue Sainte-Claire, Pont-Morens ⓛ 08.00–12.00 Tues, Fri & Sun ⓝ Bus: 6, 7, 15 to Hôtel de Ville

## TAKING A BREAK

**Au Fidèle Berger £** It's hard to resist *les cloches d'Annecy* (bells of Annecy) pralines here, where the scent of hot chocolate fills the air. If you're sweet enough already, try one of the speciality teas. ⓐ 2 rue Royale ⓣ 04 50 45 00 32 ⓛ 08.45–19.00 Tues–Sat ⓝ Bus: 6, 7, 15 to Hôtel de Ville

**Nature et Saveur £** The freshest local produce is used to create vegetarian options, fresh salads and healthy (!) desserts. ⓐ Place

des Cordeliers ☎ 04 50 45 82 29 ⦿ www.nature-saveur.com
🕓 08.30–19.00 Tues–Sat Ⓝ Bus: 6, 7, 15 to Hôtel de Ville

**Passion Gourmande £** If you're crazy about crêpes, this central
café is for you. The lunch menu offers great value and there
is a sunny terrace. ⓐ 16 rue Sainte-Claire ☎ 04 50 52 92 78
🕓 12.00–14.00, 19.00–23.00 Ⓝ Bus: 6, 7, 15 to Hôtel de Ville

## AFTER DARK

### RESTAURANTS

**Le Lilas Rose £** When it's cold outside, this canal-side bistro
dishes up hearty alpine fare like raclette, gooey fondue
and tartiflettes. ⓐ Passage de l'Évêché ☎ 04 50 45 37 08
🕓 12.00–14.00, 19.00–23.00 Ⓝ Bus: 6, 7, 15 to Hôtel de Ville

**Le Munich £** This lively brasserie and bar overlooks the Thiou
Canal. Munch on sauerkraut with sausage, knuckle of ham or
mussels and chips. There are 13 draught beers to choose from.
ⓐ 1 quai Perrière ☎ 04 50 45 02 11 ⦿ www.lemunich.com
🕓 08.00–02.00 Ⓝ Bus: 6, 7, 15 to Hôtel de Ville

**Super Panorama £** The name of this restaurant says it all: the
lake and mountain views from the terrace are as appetising
as the cuisine. Try the trout with almonds with a glass of
crisp Apremont. ⓐ 7 route du Semnoz ☎ 04 50 45 34 86
⦿ www.super-panorama.com 🕓 12.00–16.00 Mon,
12.00–22.00 Wed–Sun Ⓝ Bus: 6 to Hôtel de Police

**Auberge de Savoie ££** Fish doesn't come fresher than at this gourmet haunt, located on an attractive square opposite the Palais de l'Île. ⓐ 1 place Saint François de Sales ⓣ 04 50 45 03 05 ⓦ www.aubergedesavoie.fr ⓛ 11.30–15.00, 19.00–23.00 Thur–Mon ⓝ Bus: 6, 7, 15 to Hôtel de Ville

**La Ciboulette ££–£££** Georges Paccard cooks up a storm at this gem of a restaurant. Specialities include Pauillac lamb and filet of turbot, all served on the terrace. ⓐ 10 rue Vaugelas ⓣ 04 50 45 74 57 ⓛ 12.00–14.00, 19.00–23.00 Tues–Sat ⓝ Bus: 6, 7, 15 to Hôtel de Ville

## BARS & CLUBS

**Finn Kelly's** A favourite among Annecy's students, this relaxed Irish pub has regular jam sessions, free wireless internet, big-screen sports and a terrace where you can sip Beamish Stout. ⓐ 10 Faubourg Annonciades ⓣ 04 50 51 29 40 ⓦ www.finnkellys.com ⓛ 14.30–02.00 ⓝ Bus: 6, 7, 15 to Hôtel de Ville

**Red'z** Partygoers head for this hip club in the heart of Annecy, where DJs spin techno and house. ⓐ 4 quai Perrière ⓣ 04 50 45 02 11 ⓦ www.red-z.net ⓛ 11.00–03.00 Apr–Sept; 15.30–03.00 Oct–Mar ⓝ Bus: 6, 7, 15 to Hôtel de Ville

## ACCOMMODATION

**Annecy AJ £** A brisk uphill hike takes you to this cheery lodge-style hostel, bordering the forest and affording superb views.

It has a snug bar, spotless dorms and provides good-value meals. ⓐ 4 route du Semnoz ⓣ 04 50 45 33 19 ⓦ http://auberge-annecy.com ⓛ Apr–Oct ⓝ Bus: 6 to Hôtel de Police

**Camping Le Belvédère £** This is close enough to the lake for a dip before breakfast, only ten minutes from the beach and the Old Town. On-site facilities at this green and tranquil location include a laundry, mini-market and playground. ⓐ 8 route du Semnoz ⓣ 04 50 45 48 30 ⓔ camping@ville-annecy.fr ⓛ Apr–Oct ⓝ Bus: 6 to Hôtel de Police

**Hôtel du Château £** Nestled at the foot of the castle, this family-run hotel has an intimate feel. Rooms are simple but comfortable and offer fine views. ⓐ 16 rampe du Château ⓣ 04 50 45 27 66 ⓦ www.annecy-hotel.com ⓝ Bus: 7, 14 to Paradis

**Hôtel du Nord £** Close to the lake, this peaceful hotel is an ideal base. The rooms are decorated in warm hues and feature modern bathrooms. There is free parking and a generous breakfast buffet. ⓐ 24 rue Sommeiller ⓣ 04 50 45 08 78 ⓦ www.annecy-hotel-du-nord.com ⓝ Bus: 6, 7, 15 to Hôtel de Ville

ⓞ *Geneva's riverside tourist office*

# PRACTICAL
# information

# Directory

## GETTING THERE
### By air

Many airlines operate a frequent, direct service between Genèva-Cointrin International Airport (see page 50) and around 90 destinations including London, New York, Paris and Rome. Flybaboo, easyJet and bmibaby offer some of the best budget flights. Other key airlines include British Airways, American Airlines, Swiss and KLM.

**American Airlines** Ⓦ www.aa.com

**bmibaby** Ⓦ www.bmibaby.com

**British Airways** Ⓦ www.britishairways.com

**easyJet** Ⓦ www.easyjet.com

**Flybaboo** Ⓦ www.flybaboo.com

**KLM** Ⓦ www.klm.com

**Swiss** Ⓦ www.swiss.com

Many people are aware that air travel emits $CO_2$, which contributes to climate change. You may be interested in the possibility of lessening the environmental impact of your flight through the charity **Climate Care** (Ⓦ www.climatecare.org), which offsets your $CO_2$ by funding environmental projects around the world.

### By rail

Geneva's main station, Gare Cornavin, has excellent connections on high-speed trains to major Swiss cities including Lausanne, Bern, Basel and Zurich, as well as serving European cities including Lyon, Paris, Barcelona and Venice. Swiss Federal Railways provides detailed information on routes and timetables.

**SBB** ⓦ www.sbb.ch ⓣ 0900 300 300

The monthly *Thomas Cook European Rail Timetable* has up-to-date schedules for European international and national train services.

**Thomas Cook European Rail Timetable** ⓣ (UK) 01733 416477, (USA) 1 800 322 3834 ⓦ www.thomascookpublishing.com

## By road

International and long-distance buses depart from Geneva's main bus station on place Dorcière, operating to destinations including Lyon, Rome and London. For details of bus services in and around Geneva see ⓦ www.tpg.ch. **Eurolines** (ⓦ www.eurolines.com) also offers international bus services to the city.

🔺 *A SNCF train pulls in to Gare Cornavin, the central railway station*

Switzerland's roads are well maintained, driving is on the right and international signs are used. The speed limit is strictly enforced, with cameras operating on most stretches of motorway and speeding offences often subject to hefty on-the-spot fines. To drive on Switzerland's motorways, you'll need to purchase a Vignette (toll sticker) to display in the front windscreen. On a clear run, you can reach Lausanne in 45 minutes, Lyon in 1 hour 30 minutes and Zurich in 2 hours 30 minutes.

## ENTRY FORMALITIES

EU, Australian, Canadian, New Zealand, South African and United States citizens must have a valid passport to enter Switzerland, but do not require a visa for stays of fewer than 90 days. If you are arriving from countries other than these, you may need a visa and should contact your consulate or embassy up to three months before departure. The **Swiss Federal Department of Foreign Affairs** (ⓦ www.eda.admin.ch) provides more information on entry requirements.

It is usually free to import goods from a non-EU country, but you should check restrictions on the imports of tobacco, perfume and alcohol. Further information is available at ⓦ www.ezv.admin.ch

## MONEY

Switzerland's currency is the Swiss franc (CHF), divided up into 100 rappen or centimes. Coins are in denominations of CHF5, 2 and 1, and 50, 20, 10 and 5 centimes. There are banknotes of 10, 20, 50, 100, 200, 500 and 1,000 francs. Many of Geneva's restaurants, hotels and shops also accept euros, but remember that you will be given the change back in Swiss francs.

Central Geneva has plenty of ATMs where you can withdraw cash with your credit or debit card 24 hours a day, although it's worth checking whether the bank imposes a fee. Most banks open 08.30–16.30 Monday to Friday.

There are bureaux de change in banks, the main train station and the airport. Traveller's cheques can be cashed in most bureaux de change, banks, travel agencies and hotels. Banks generally offer the best rates. Visa, MasterCard, Diners Club and American Express are widely accepted.

## HEALTH, SAFETY & CRIME

Geneva is a clean and safe city to visit, and there are no particular health risks. No immunisations or health certificates are required and the tap water is safe to drink.

While Switzerland has one of the best standards of medical care in the world, treatment can be expensive, so it's wise to invest in a good health insurance policy before visiting. EU citizens are entitled to free or reduced-cost emergency health care with a valid European Health Insurance Card (EHIC), which entitles you to state medical treatment but does not cover repatriation or long-term illness.

Pharmacies can treat minor ailments and are usually open 07.45–18.30 Monday to Friday and 08.00–17.00 Saturday. The **Geneva Pharmacies Association** (ⓦ www.pharmacies-geneve.ch) lists 24-hour pharmacies on their website. Your hotel should be able to arrange for you to see an English-speaking doctor, if necessary.

The crime rate in Geneva is low, so you shouldn't experience any problems during your stay. However, pickpockets may operate in key tourist areas, so it's wise to keep an eye on your possessions. If you are the victim of a crime, you should inform the police by calling 117 (see *Emergencies*, page 138).

## OPENING HOURS
Banks open 08.30–16.30 Monday to Friday. All close at weekends, but many have 24-hour ATMs. Most shops open 09.00–19.00 Monday to Saturday; smaller boutiques often close for lunch. Shopping malls and department stores stay open until 21.00 on Thursdays.

## TOILETS
There are clean public toilets in the centre of Geneva, with most offering baby-changing facilities and access to disabled travellers. You'll need 50 centimes to use the city's automatic, self-cleaning toilets. Most cafés, restaurants and some department stores have free toilets for customers.

## CHILDREN
Extremely clean and easy to negotiate, this family-friendly city has a range of attractions to keep children amused. There is usually a 50 per cent reduction for children, and kids are welcome in most restaurants and cafés.

**Bains des Pâquis** The Right Bank's pier is a relaxed spot for families to enjoy a picnic and swim (see page 76).

**Bois de la Bâtie (Bâtie Woods)** Children will love to explore the caves, gorges and woodlands. There's also a splash pool and playground. ⓐ Bâtie Ⓝ Bus: 2, 11 to Bâtie

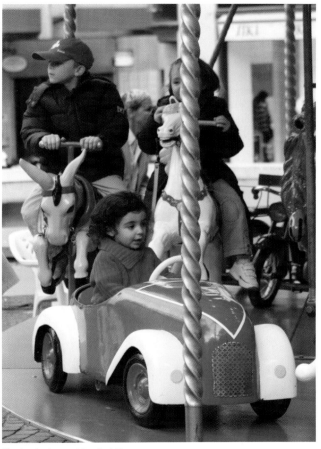

🔺 *There's plenty of fun for kids*

## GENEVA CARD
Families can save by purchasing a Geneva Card, offering free access to the public transport network and entry to many top museums and attractions, plus reductions in some shops and restaurants. The card is available for 24 or 72 hours and can be purchased from the tourist information centre (see page 137).

**Genève-Plage (Geneva Beach)** Tots enjoy the paddling pool, sandpit and slides here, while teens head for the Olympic Swimming Pool, diving boards and volleyball court (see page 35).
**Mini-train** In summer, a mini-train chugs through Geneva's streets to take in the key sights. ⓐ Rotonde du Mont-Blanc ⓣ 022 781 04 04 ⓦ www.sttr.ch ⓛ 10.00–dusk Mar–Oct ⓝ Bus: 8 to Chantepoulet
**Vivarium Lausanne** Children can spot crocodiles, turtles, anacondas and lizards at one of Europe's leading vivariums. ⓐ 82 chemin de Boissonnet, Lausanne ⓣ 021 652 72 94 ⓦ www.vivarium-lausanne.ch ⓛ 14.00–17.30 Mon–Fri, 10.00–17.30 Sat & Sun ⓝ Bus: 14 to Mont. Admission charge

## COMMUNICATION
### Internet
Wireless internet access (Wi-Fi) has become widespread in Geneva with many cafés, restaurants, bars, hotels and even petrol stations offering the service. The following website gives details on free hotspots in Switzerland ⓦ www.freespots.ch.

There are a handful of internet cafés in the centre of Geneva that offer a high-speed broadband connection. Expect to pay between CHF5 and CHF10 for an hour online.

**Charly's Check Point** Open 24 hours, this offers internet access as well as services like scanning and faxing. ⓐ 7 rue de Fribourg ⓣ 022 901 13 13 ⓦ www.charlys.com ⓛ 09.00–00.00 Mon–Sat, 14.00–22.00 Sun ⓝ Tram: 13, 15 to Cornavin

**Cyber-Café 3000** This cheery café has a reliable internet connection, plus printers and scanners. ⓐ 2 rue Henri-Christine ⓣ 022 320 74 55 ⓛ 11.00–21.00 ⓝ Tram: 13 to Pont-d'Arve

**Las Vegas Mont-Blanc Cyberland** Conveniently located near the main station. ⓐ 26 rue du Mont-Blanc ⓣ 022 738 57 44 ⓝ Tram: 13, 15 to Cornavin

**Laundrenet** Doubling as a laundrette, this place offers a high-speed internet connection, scanner and colour printing. ⓐ 83 rue de la Servette ⓣ 022 734 83 83 ⓦ www.laundrenet.ch

**TELEPHONING SWITZERLAND**
Dial 00 41 for Switzerland, then 22 for Geneva followed by the seven-digit number.

**TELEPHONING ABROAD**
To call out of Switzerland, simply dial 00 followed by the country code and the local number.

**Directory Enquiries** ⓣ 1811
**International Operator** ⓣ 1141

🕐 12.00–22.00 Mon & Wed, 09.00–22.00 Tues & Thur, 09.00–21.00 Fri & Sat, 12.00–20.00 Sun 🚌 Bus: 9 to Poterie

## Phones

Geneva's modern public telephone boxes are simple to use and rates reasonable. Only some phones accept coins, so you'll probably need to buy a prepaid phone card or use your credit card. Many of the phone booths in Geneva allow you to send SMS messages and emails also.

## Post

You can purchase stamps in post offices and some newsagents. The main post office in the city centre is on rue du Mont-Blanc. Ⓦ www.swisspost.ch

## ELECTRICITY

Switzerland's electricity system is very reliable. It is 220 volts, 50 hertz (round, three-pin plugs). Adaptors and transformers are available for visitors.

## TRAVELLERS WITH DISABILITIES

Geneva caters to travellers with special needs. Most of the city's key attractions are accessible for visitors with disabilities, including MAMCO, the Palace of Nations and the International Red Cross Museum; many offer concessions (*tarif réduit*) or free entry. If notified in advance, Swiss Federal Railways (SBB) can assist wheelchair users and passengers with reduced mobility. ☎ 0800 007 102

**Australia & New Zealand** Accessibility Ⓦ www.accessibility.com.au;
Disabled Persons Assembly ❶ 04 801 9100 Ⓦ www.dpa.org.nz
**Switzerland** Mobility International Switzerland (MIS)
ⓐ 4 Froburgstrasse, Olten ❶ 062 206 88 35 Ⓦ www.mis-ch.ch
**UK & Ireland** British Council of Disabled People (BCDP)
❶ 01332 295551 Ⓦ www.bcodp.org.uk
**US & Canada** Society for Accessible Travel & Hospitality (SATH)
ⓐ 347 Fifth Ave, New York ❶ 212 447 7284 Ⓦ www.sath.org;
Access-Able Ⓦ www.access-able.com

## TOURIST INFORMATION

**Geneva Tourism** ⓐ 18 rue du Mont-Blanc ❶ 022 909 70 00
Ⓦ www.geneve-tourisme.ch 🕙 10.00–18.00 Mon, 09.00–18.00
Tues–Sat, winter; 10.00–18.00 Mon, 09.00–18.00 Tues–Sun, summer
**Lausanne Tourism** ⓐ 9 place de la Gare ❶ 021 613 73 73
Ⓦ www.lausanne-tourisme.ch 🕙 09.00–19.00
**Annecy Tourist Office** ⓐ 1 rue Jean-Jaurès ❶ 04 50 45 00 33
Ⓦ www.lac-annecy.com 🕙 09.00–12.00, 13.45–18.00 Mon–Sat
**Carouge Tourist Information** Ⓦ www.carouge.ch

# Emergencies

### EMERGENCY NUMBERS

The following are national free emergency numbers:

**Police** 🛈 117

**Fire** 🛈 118

**Ambulance** 🛈 144

**Emergency** 🛈 112

**Breakdown** 🛈 140

**On-call doctors** 🛈 022 748 49 50

When you dial the Europe-wide emergency number 🛈 112, ask for the service you require and give details of where you are, what the emergency is and the number of the phone you are using. The operator will connect you to the service you need.

### MEDICAL SERVICES

It is strongly recommended to have a valid health insurance policy before travelling to Switzerland. EU citizens are entitled to free or reduced-cost emergency health care with a European Health Insurance Card (EHIC). For details on late-opening pharmacies, call 🛈 022 306 08 50 or visit 🆆 www.pharmacies-geneve.ch for a list of 24-hour pharmacies.

The centrally located **Geneva University Hospital** (HUG, 🅰 24 rue Micheli-du-Crest 🛈 022 372 33 11 🆆 www.hug-ge.ch) provides emergency treatment.

### POLICE

Open 24 hours a day, seven days a week, the police station at Gare Cornavin can be reached by calling 🛈 022 388 61 00.

## EMERGENCY PHRASES

| **Help!** | **Fire!** | **Stop!** |
|---|---|---|
| Au secours! | Au feu! | Stop! |
| *Ossercoor!* | *Oh fur!* | *Stop!* |

**Call an ambulance/a doctor/the police/the fire service!**
Appelez une ambulance/un médecin/la police/les pompiers!
*Ahperleh ewn ahngbewlahngss/ang medesang/lah poleess/
leh pompeeyeh!*

## EMBASSIES & CONSULATES

**Australia** @ 2 chemin des Fins, Bern ☎ 022 799 91 00
ⓦ www.australia.ch 🕒 09.00–17.00 Mon–Fri

**Canada** @ 88 Kirchenfeldstrasse, Bern ☎ 031 357 32 00
ⓦ www.bern.gc.ca 🕒 08.00–12.00, 13.00–17.00 Mon–Thur,
08.00–13.30 Fri

**Ireland** @ 68 Kirchenfeldstrasse, Bern ☎ 031 352 14 42
ⓔ berneembassy@dfa.ie 🕒 09.00–17.00 Mon–Fri

**South Africa** @ 29 Alpenstrasse, Bern ☎ 031 350 13 13
ⓦ www.southafrica.ch 🕒 08.00–12.30, 13.30–17.15 Mon–Thur,
08.00–12.00, 13.00–15.00 Fri

**UK** @ 37–39 rue de Vermont, Bern ☎ 022 918 24 18
ⓦ www.britishembassy.gov.uk 🕒 08.30–12.30, 14.00–17.00
Mon–Fri

**USA** @ 95 Jubilaumsstrasse, Bern ☎ 031 357 72 34
ⓦ http://bern.usembassy.gov 🕒 09.00–11.30 Mon–Fri

# SPOTTED YOUR NEXT CITY BREAK?

... then these CitySpots will have you in the know in no time, wherever you're heading.

Covering 100 cities worldwide, these vibrant pocket guides are packed with practical listings and imaginative suggestions, making sure you get the most out of your break, whatever your taste or budget.

| | | |
|---|---|---|
| Aarhus | Geneva | Paris |
| Amsterdam | Genoa | Pisa |
| Antwerp | Glasgow | Prague |
| Athens | Gothenburg | Porto |
| Bangkok | Granada | Reims |
| Barcelona | Hamburg | Reykjavik |
| Belfast | Hanover | Riga |
| Belgrade | Helsinki | Rome |
| Berlin | Hong Kong | Rotterdam |
| Biarritz | Istanbul | Salzburg |
| Bilbao | Kiev | San Francisco |
| Bologna | Krakow | Sarajevo |
| Bordeaux | Kuala Lumpur | Seville |
| Bratislava | Leipzig | Singapore |
| Bruges | Lille | Sofia |
| Brussels | Lisbon | Split |
| Bucharest | Liverpool | Stockholm |
| Budapest | Ljubljana | Strasbourg |
| Cairo | London | St Petersburg |
| Cape Town | Los Angeles | Tallinn |
| Cardiff | Lyon | Tirana |
| Cologne | Madrid | Tokyo |
| Copenhagen | Marrakech | Toulouse |
| Cork | Marseilles | Turin |
| Delhi | Milan | Valencia |
| Dubai | Monte Carlo | Venice |
| Dublin | Moscow | Verona |
| Dubrovnik | Munich | Vienna |
| Düsseldorf | Naples | Vilnius |
| Edinburgh | New York City | Warsaw |
| Fez | Nice | Zagreb |
| Florence | Oslo | Zurich |
| Frankfurt | Palermo | |
| Gdansk | Palma | |

Available from all good bookshops, your local Thomas Cook travel store or browse and buy online at www.thomascookpublishing.com

**Thomas Cook** Publishing

Editorial/project management: Lisa Plumridge
Copy editor: Monica Guy
Layout/DTP: Alison Rayner

The publishers would like to thank the following individuals
and organisations for supplying their copyright photographs
for this book: Andy Christiani, pages 1, 7, 9, 17, 18, 34, 42–3, 65, 77,
80–1, 92, 94, 105 & 110; Paul Downey, page 25; Manotel, page 39;
Pictures Colour Library, pages 45 & 121; Tom Taylor, page 129;
World Pictures/Photoshot, pages 103, 117 & 118; Jonathan Smith,
all others.

## Send your thoughts to
# books@thomascook.com

- Found a great bar, club, shop or must-see sight that we don't feature?
- Like to tip us off about any information that needs a little updating?
- Want to tell us what you love about this handy little guidebook and
  more importantly how we can make it even handier?

Then here's your chance to tell all! Send us ideas, discoveries and
recommendations today and then look out for your valuable input
in the next edition of this title.

Email the above address (stating the title) or write to:
CitySpots Series Editor, Thomas Cook Publishing, PO Box 227,
Coningsby Road, Peterborough PE3 8SB, UK.